A Nickel's Worth of HOPE

By ANDRÉ VANDENBERG
Condensed by Bob Terrell

PQK116045

A
Nickel's
Worth
of
HOPE

André Vandenberg

Condensed by Bob Terrell

Eagles' Wings Publications,
P.O. Box 877, Mountain Home, N.C. 28758.

This book is gratefully dedicated to
my wife, Connie,
who stood faithfully by my side through many trials.

This special Billy Graham Evangelistic Association
edition is published with permission.

Acknowledgements

Many people are involved in the making of a book. That is why I wish to express my heartfelt appreciation to those who have had a definite part in making this book a reality:

To my daughters Ingrid and Marianne who carefully weeded out the grammatical errors and streamlined the flow of words.

To Ms. M. J. Finke and Ms. Jeleta Fryman I especially owe a debt of gratitude for their editorial suggestions and corrections.

To Lorraine Jones, my thanks and appreciation for retyping the manuscript.

To Rudy D. Morrell and Reverend Calvin Thielman, two special friends to whom I am deeply grateful for their unwavering support and efforts to encourage me in completing the manuscript.

To Richard Van Wingerden, my son-in-law, whose financial support made the publication of this book possible.

The Author

CONTENTS

PROLOGUE

The day André Vandenberg died he climbed a mountain in Honduras. Climbing mountains was nothing for this man who had dedicated his life to helping people find Christ as their Savior and improve their economic well-being.

As a young man, Vandenberg had survived a death camp in Nazi Germany and after the war had walked and hitchhiked from his native Holland to South Africa. It was a journey of two years that took him through the burning sands of the Sahara. When Ruth Graham asked André how one hitchhikes through the Sahara, he laughed and said, "There are ways."

That day in Honduras, he had taken four visitors from Kansas up the mountain to a village where they had started a new church. The climb was hard, but André did not complain. He rested once—and used the break to share the Gospel with all who passed by!

That afternoon they descended the mountain to the village of Lagas, where André and his wife, Connie, lived in a mission home. From that village, André had established churches in four other nearby villages. He had a topographical map of that mountainous area of Honduras, and on it he had printed the words of Caleb: "Give me therefore this mountain."

André's days were long and full. He evangelized throughout the area. He loved the people. He supervised a business in which local villagers grew ornamental plants, providing them with badly needed paychecks. He had a pickup truck which he used as an ambulance to take villagers to the hospital. He counseled the people on any subject in which he felt qualified. He was even a "banker," loaning money with no thought of ever getting it back.

He gave his own clothing to the villagers. People came constantly to the Vandenberg door to say, "I have no shoes, nothing to wear," and André would go to his closet and start pulling things out.

"I remember one man coming to our door," said André's daughter, Marianne, "and saying he didn't have a shirt. Daddy went to the closet and started to pull out one of his few shirts, and I heard Mom say, 'Oh, no, you can't give him that one.' So my father began to unbutton the shirt he was wearing to give it to the man."

André Vandenberg was a totally selfless man who knew the feelings of the people to whom he ministered. For he had known hard times himself—extremely hard times.

That evening after climbing the mountain, André and the four men from Kansas finished working in the village about 7:30 and André said to Connie, "I'm tired. I'm going to bed."

As he lay in bed, his face showed the strain of hard days. "Connie," he said, "please pray for me. I don't feel well. There is something hurting in my chest."

Connie prayed over him, but she could see that he needed help. He was perspiring profusely and was obviously in pain. She asked the four men to come upstairs and pray for André. She asked André if he wanted to go to the hospital and he said yes, but a few minutes later he changed his mind.

"Connie," he whispered, "I don't really want to go. The hurt is so bad."

Connie insisted, however, and the men lifted André onto a mattress in the enclosed back of his truck. Connie navigated as they headed into the fog. The track wound up the mountain and around a cliff before descending to the hospital.

One of the men in the truck camper with André gave him a nitroglycerin tablet, and when he arrived at the hospital forty-five minutes later he seemed better. Attendants took x-rays and ran tests. Someone told Connie that an American doctor was in the hospital, and she ran and found her. An American doctor, she thought, would know more about treating a heart ailment, because Hondurans do not have such a high incidence of heart trouble as Americans.

Just before attendants took André to his room, he said to Connie, "I want you to go home. It has been a long day for you and you look tired."

"No, André," Connie insisted. "I am staying with you."

He said, "I want you to take care of your health." And then, "Who will take those men to the airport?" meaning the four from Kansas, who were scheduled to leave the following day. To the end, André thought of others.

In his room, André started to put on his pajamas.

"Here, let me help you," Connie said.

"No, no," he said, "I can do it."

He fell on the floor and was gone.

The date was September 14, 1989.

Thus ended the incredible journey of André Vandenberg.

Bob Terrell

... Chapter One: ...

Chapter One:

THE VIOLENT YEARS

Sounds of groaning and extreme anguish penetrated my semi-conscious mind. I struggled to bring my surroundings into focus. Painfully, I turned my head from side to side and saw emaciated bodies with shaved heads. I saw shivering men clad only in striped shirts, and soon realized that I, too, was wearing only a striped shirt.

In spite of the fever burning in my bones, I was cold. My head throbbed as though it would burst. I had no notion of time or place. I tried to remember, but nothing came to me. I couldn't even remember my own name or nationality.

Again I looked at the other men. Their bald heads had odd shapes; their writhing, feverish bodies looked so thin and frail.

Loud explosions sounded from beyond the wall, but I couldn't identify their source.

I looked at what was left of my body: My arms and legs were mere bones covered with skin. There was excruciating pain when I made the slightest move. Then I discovered the reason: My bones had worn through my skin!

My bed was a thin straw mat on the concrete. *What am I doing on this cold concrete floor?* I wondered. *Why am I suffering so much pain?*

One thing I *did* know, and with a strange certainty: I knew there was a God, and that He was an awesome God! The very atmosphere around me was pervaded with His presence. I was aware of an indescribable vastness. *Whoever I am, I must be passing on to something unknown, and the threshold is not far off.*

In that eternity I knew I would have to meet God. That was a most frightening thought, because I knew I was not ready to meet Him.

How was it possible that I knew without a doubt there was a God and that I had to face Him—even while being unconscious of my own identity? I was so far gone that my body made no more demands. I hadn't eaten for weeks. I had no physical desires; all normal functions of the body had apparently ceased. But I was conscious of a spiritual world unknown to me till that moment. I could almost grasp it. Though my body was nearly dead, my spirit was so very much alive.

Looking at my chest, I noticed tiny creatures of various colors crawling about. Lice! How interesting they looked, making their way to a new hideout. Maybe they had lost interest in the sick blood of a dying man.

The skeletons around me stirred and moaned. *Why do these men have to go through this ordeal? Why is the all-present God so real and at the same time so terrifying to me? Why can't I remember my name?*

The explosions outside became even louder. One could tell by a whistling sound that the next violent outburst was due in a matter of seconds. Loud thuds hit the building, followed by the terrible screaming of the wounded.

Day turned to night and night to day again. I tossed and turned in pain and half-slumber, trying to understand why it had become so quiet. Suddenly, a piercing scream cut through the silence, penetrating the marrow of my bones, and my mind began opening to what was taking place. All the lost events trickled back into my memory. The long years in prisons and concentration camps—the hunger, the filth, the deprivations and humiliations.

It must now be early spring of 1945, and I am somewhere in Germany.

Instinctively, a prayer flowed from my lips: "God, I know You are out there. You know I haven't lived yet. Give me another chance. Just give me another chance, and I will serve You forever."

How very much I meant that prayer and that promise!

I continued my reflections, piecing together the incidents that had brought me to these terrible circumstances.

I remembered my mom and dad bringing up five children with discipline and love. In the years preceding the war, we lived in a small village in western Holland. We could see the clouds of war gathering over Europe, but like so many others had the misguided idea that the conflict would not touch us. Holland would remain neutral.

But the Nazis did come, in the spring of 1940. I was nearly seventeen when our village was overrun, and my heart gradually filled with hatred for the conquering armies. Giving vent to our feelings, my friends and I sought ways to sabotage the forces plundering our land.

The call of the Free World became stronger each day. Young men were needed to liberate their countries from the Nazis. I decided I could best serve my country by joining the Dutch Free Forces in England. I could repay the invaders with the same kind of treatment they had dished out to us. "An eye for an eye; a tooth for a tooth!"

But how could I escape to England? Taking the direct route meant crossing the North Sea by canoe, a two-hundred-mile trip. Though we lived on the coast, the beaches were heavily guarded.

Failing to find an escape route by sea, my attention turned to another possibility: to reach England through southern Europe. If a Dutchman could reach Spain or Portugal, which were neutral, he could present himself at any Dutch consulate. All Dutch consuls were under orders to send every young man eighteen or older on to England for military service.

I mapped out a route, and in October 1941 started for the Free World, heading by bicycle for the Belgian border. The first miles were easy, riding through the flat Dutch countryside. Arriving near the border post the next evening, I followed a narrow path across a number of meadows and ditches and encountered some Belgian farmers. They assured me that I had reached Belgian soil safely, so I headed again for the highway and the next country, France. When the hills of Belgium made bicycling more strenuous, I sold my bike and continued on foot, by bus, and by train.

In France I was able to avoid the Germans, the French police, and the border guards. At that time in 1941, France was still divided into German-occupied France and Free France, whose Vichy government was collaborating with the Nazis. Arriving in Chalon sur Saone, I knew that the division between the two Frances was somewhere close, and with the utmost care I advanced through town. Soon it became clear to me that the large river Saone had become a natural border between free and occupied France.

Intently I studied the other side, the river, and the possibility of crossing it unobserved. It was about one o'clock in the afternoon and too early to try anything. The best plan was to wait until dark. In the meantime, I could search for the best possible crossing point. Following the river, I came to a bridge and saw that no one was guarding it. The area across the river was surrounded by barbed wire. In the distance I spotted a roadblock, heavily manned by German soldiers. My pulse throbbed faster.

While crossing the bridge I discovered on the right side some trees and thick bushes. A perfect hiding place! I would have to hide until it was dark enough, and then I could climb the barbed wire fence and run for freedom.

Unfortunately, the Nazis had anticipated freedom-loving people with ideas like mine and had installed an observation post in the first home across the river. As I left the bridge on the far end, inside the observation post an observer reported to an officer that a young man had just crossed the bridge and was heading for the bushes. Within seconds a German officer was dispatched. I hid as well as I could, but there was no way to escape him. The river was on one side, barbed wire on the other, and in a moment the officer pointed a gun toward me.

"Hands up!"

Any move on my part would have been fatal. I raised my hands, he shoved the barrel of his gun into my back and marched me to a military post. There I was stripped, scrutinized, and interrogated. German soldiers joked and poked fun at me. My map, indicating the route to the Free World, incriminated me. I hoped for a chance to escape, but the post swarmed with troops.

That same night I was dumped into prison. A German sergeant opened a cell door on the second floor, shoved me in, and locked the door behind me. He seemed content with his last catch of the day.

The rattling of the keys ceased, and hearing the retreating footsteps of the sergeant I felt entirely alone in a strange, new world.

"Bon soir, bon soir." I strained my eyes in the half-dark to see three unshaven, smelly Frenchmen who welcomed a new cell mate into the already overcrowded quarters of nine by twelve feet. My French was limited, so communication was nearly zero, but it didn't take much knowledge of any language to understand that there was no comfort in the cell. There were no cots, no blankets, only a dirty concrete floor to lie on.

During the next few days as I tried to acclimate myself to prison life, I became acutely aware that, as a "political prisoner" I had no rights to human decency. No spoons or other eating utensils were issued. Watery soup had to be drunk from dirty pans. In the courtyard where prisoners assembled twice a day, there was only one faucet. The corner of the courtyard contained another convenience—two holes in the ground for latrines, often plugged up.

There was never to be a shower or change of clothing in this prison; neither were we ever given a haircut or shave. The way we entered was the way we stayed. I picked up a discarded horse blanket encrusted with human feces. It was at least something against the cold.

What hope was there for an end to all this? England, which so far had survived the onslaught of the Luftwaffe, was tending to her own wounds. The United States was not yet a combat force in the war. Russia, invaded only a few months before, was retreating toward Siberia. Escape from this hell hole was my only hope, however slim.

Two months went by, then a German military court in

Chalon sur Saone found me guilty of *feind begunstigung* (favoritism toward the enemy). My sentence of ten years at hard labor was considered lenient. It would surely squelch any trace of freedom-fire in me.

"Think of it this way," one of the officers said, "if you don't die, you'll be out by the time you're twenty-eight."

My future looked bleak. A young Belgian in a cell next to mine apparently felt the same way. Tired of such a meaningless existence, he hanged himself. A Frenchman across the hall had been sentenced to ten years at hard labor. One afternoon I was ordered to clean up his cell. There were pools of blood everywhere. He had smashed a small window pane overhead and used the broken glass to cut both wrists and his throat. As a final act of defiance, he had dipped his fingers in his own blood and in large red letters had written his last message to the world: VIVE LA MORT! VIVE DE GAULLE!

Finally came the time to move prisoners with long sentences to another prison. I began the long odyssey through France and Germany, handcuffed to another young Dutchman and guarded by three soldiers. We spent a few days in one prison, a few weeks in another, then were moved again. Days of hunger and cold gripped us. Kicked around and insulted, a spectacle to civilians, we were sent off to yet another place of confinement.

I spent the first year and a half of incarceration in six different prisons and camps. In the summer of 1943, I arrived—apparently to stay—in Siegburg, Germany.

All newcomers had to don the uniforms of convicts—short, black coats, and pants with yellow stripes. Jews had the added insignia of the Star of Bethlehem. We were given wooden galoshes, which made us stumble. Between three and four thousand men crowded this camp built for about one thousand. At least seventeen different nationalities were represented among us. Apparently every European nation had to sample the supreme degradation of Nazi imprisonment and torture.

Though never very religious, I found myself looking for signs of Christianity. As a child my parents had taken me to an orthodox but cold church, and there we were instructed in the

Bible. At times I had pondered the miracles of the Old and New Testaments. Why did they occur then and not now? Or were miracles still occurring? Or had they ever, really?

Actually, I did not know Christ and was indefensible against the evidence before me, now that the Nazis were in the forefront of all who claimed any religious belief: On the buckles of Nazi belts was clearly engraved, Gott mit uns. And He surely did seem to be with them, judging from the political and military blessings they enjoyed.

While at Siegburg I became the cell mate of a strange character with a very different approach to life. He was someone I had heard much about but had never seen: Mr. Helteman, who had been a communist party leader in one of Europe's major cities. This thin, drawn young man of about thirty came toward me with an outstretched hand. His first question surprised me.

"Are you a Christian?"

I couldn't believe my ears. I stared at him incredulously, unable to answer. Finally I managed to nod my head.

"Well, I'm a Christian too," he said.

Of all the nerve, I thought. This from a rabid communist!

"I know who you are," I managed to say. "And being who you are, I'd rather you left the subject of religion alone."

He laughed. "That I will not do," he said. "I fully expect to tell you a great deal about myself, including my religious experience."

In the months that followed I did indeed hear Mr. Helteman's story, and from what I observed of his behavior did not doubt it. The SS guards, having heard of his communist background, had sought him out one day and beat him mercilessly. They had decided to extract the names of his associates and details of their activities. At last he made up a saga of lies, which were duly recorded.

Not content with that record, the interrogators beat him more severely a week or two later. This time he invented new lies. Soon afterward, a third beating came. This time the SS really worked him over. When at last they thought he was ready for a true admission of guilt—with teeth knocked out, face virtually pulped, and one arm and several ribs broken—they once more demanded the facts about the other members of his apparatus. Barely able to talk, he was still able to lie, to protect the lives of his comrades still at large. And once more the guards recorded what he had to say.

After this beating, Mr. Helteman was put in a cell with a Jehovah's Witness. It was not long until the Jehovah's Witness was taken away permanently. But he left behind a small New Testament. With nothing else in hand, and probably to take his mind off the next beating, Mr. Helteman began reading. It was all new to him. He read eagerly through Matthew, Mark, Luke, and John. He paced the cell and thought. Again he picked up the little black book and read and reread. The story that unfolded began to grip him.

The more he read, the more he wanted to know and the more he was convinced that he had at last found the truth.

And he wanted to be totally committed to what he had learned from the New Testament. Knowing his tormentors would soon interrogate him again, he faced a nearly impossible choice: If he told the truth to the SS, he would be betraying his friends; but if he lied again, he felt he would be betraying Christ!

There and then he decided to tell the truth and leave the outcome to "the God of the little black book."

"Lord," he prayed aloud, "I know You want me to tell the truth, no matter what happens. Protect those friends of mine, even if I have to disclose their names in order to be true to You."

Hardly had he made that resolution when the cell door opened and he was taken away for his fourth beating. This time he told the truth, but the Nazis thought he was still lying. They sentenced him to fifteen years at hard labor.

I watched this strange and different person for possible flaws in his new life. Noticing that he was saving one slice of bread each day out of a virtual starvation diet, I inquired, "What are you saving bread for?"

"This bread is for those who need it in the sick bay," he said. "Have you ever seen those diseased prisoners? They need all the help they can get." He then added with conviction, "God will take care of me."

"Be sensible now," I answered. "You'll need that bread yourself. Each of us should take care of himself."

He looked straight at me and asked sharply, "Are you a Christian? And do you mean to imply that you can only be a Christian on the outside, but here in this hideous hell not have concern for the needs of others?"

I tried to think of a cutting answer, but couldn't.

Toward the end of the war, the situation in Siegburg became even more desperate. Many of the men slipped away into eternity—some from hunger, some from diseases, and some just gave up.

One day a well-known French engineer came to talk about the end of the war. "You know as well as I do," he predicted accurately, "that the Nazi leaders will decree that no prisoner shall fall alive into the hands of the Allies. So we will have to do something about that ourselves."

"That's dangerous talk, Monsieur," I replied. "That kind of talk can cost your life. You should know that we can't trust even some of our prisoner 'friends' here. Some of these men would sell their souls for a cigarette."

"Go ahead and betray me if you feel like that," the engineer answered softly.

"You know I would not do that," I responded with indignation.

"That's the reason we came to you," he said, "because we trust you. I have been asked to form an underground organization of all the prisoners we can rely on. We'll organize ourselves into several defense groups. Then we'll be able to take over the camp when the time comes."

The engineer paused to observe my reaction.

"Who are the 'we' you keep talking about?" I asked. "Name some of those who are already in your group."

"That's just the point," he said. "If you volunteer to become part of us, the only person you'll ever know in this defense structure is me. You'll be getting orders from me. Then, if you feel like becoming a deceiver, you can betray only me, for I will be the only contact man. The same goes for everyone else."

9

Again he paused, letting me digest his proposal.

"What do you expect me to do if I join your organization?"

"Are you prepared to commit murder?" he asked coldly. Though I had seen death at close range, I was not prepared to look at things in the same light as this man. However, what would happen if the Nazis did try to slaughter the camp survivors? Would I stand idly by and not defend my fellow prisoners?

The man in front of me must have guessed my thoughts.

"Remember, when I say 'commit murder' I really mean mass murder! We have to be prepared for the worst. We're already in possession of some weapons and we plan to steal more. Can we count on you?"

I faced the most difficult moral issue of my twenty years; there seemed much logical reasoning in the engineer's proposal.

"Yes," I said, "I will help." I reached and pressed the Frenchman's hand. He was right. We had to stand together if we wanted to stay alive, even at the cost of so many German lives. This kind of decision, I believed, was not up to God; I had to make it for myself.

Time wore on, and the Allied forces advanced from the west, east, and south, crushing the Third Reich. We heard little news from our guards; wisely, they kept their mouths shut. But we had found other ways to keep reasonably well informed.

Now and then a German officer's car came into camp for repairs. These cars often were equipped with a wonderful treasure—a radio. We spotted this specialty immediately, but the SS recognized the value of radios to us and made it a point to outsmart *diesen schweinhunde* (these pig-dogs) by removing the car's battery right away. Besides, there was always a guard to keep prisoners in line. They left us little chance to tune in on wavelengths that could bring rays of hope. But we were so hungry for news from the Free World that we didn't let any opportunity pass.

There were usually several trucks in the shop for repairs. So when an officer's car would come in, stripped of its battery, it would be surrounded by trucks—with good batteries! We brought two cables from the nearest truck, placed them under boards on the floor, to be out of sight, then connected them to the car with the radio. Four prisoners stood watch, working on nearby trucks. At any sign of danger, the watcher who spotted it hammered on the mudguard of his truck and the prisoner under the truck with the battery disconnected the cables immediately.

Finding something to repair in the officer's car was the easiest part. If the car was in perfect condition, I would rip a tear in the seat, and because I worked as an upholsterer in the garage, I would be called in to repair the damage. The opportunity to turn on the radio and zero in on the news was right there.

During my years in prison I had learned a few languages well, and could pick up various Free World broadcasts. Faithfully, my prisoner friends watched over me while I neatly repaired tears in the seats of many officers' cars . . . and engraved in my mind the positions of the Allied armies. Words could never express the excitement of hearing the voices of people who were actually free, commenting on the progress of the war.

Once we obtained such information, passing it on was the next hurdle. We scribbled the latest news on four small pieces of paper—one in French, one in Russian, one in German, and one in Dutch. Then we handed the "newsletters" to friends with the oral message, "As soon as you have read this, pass it to someone else. If the next person, or the next one down the line, is not acquainted with someone trustworthy to give the news to, then send this paper back the same route." When the smudgy little sheets reached us once more, we destroyed them.

I marveled that in a matter of minutes the entire camp buzzed with news. It was ironic also that a day or so later some prisoner would come and share with me the latest war stories. The day-old version was usually so distorted and exaggerated that I could hardly recognize it. The mind of a prisoner surely runs wild at the slightest gleam of hope.

As news from the outside world became brighter, the situation inside our prison grew steadily worse. Insufficient food rations became smaller still, and our workload became heavier. Our water had become contaminated. Death claimed more victims each day. Our clothes had not been washed for six months, and fleas and lice bred in them. Diseases spread, and when friends around us died the cause of death was often guesswork. One could easily recognize the victims of tuberculosis, or of hunger, or those who suffered from malfunction of the kidneys. The bloated bodies of prisoners in the last category writhed in pain for weeks and then death came horribly.

Some of the prisoners worked in a nearby artificial wool factory. They were forced to labor over tubs with poisonous liquid through which the artificial threads were squeezed. Many lost their eyesight from contact with the poison. Others' minds were affected. They would start to crawl on hands and feet, then barking like dogs would bite anyone near. It was heartbreaking to hear these humans bark through the night. Bullets usually put an end to them.

At the beginning of 1945 a mysterious disease stalked the camp. No one knew what it was but we guessed it had something to do with lice. To make sure that we were not the only ones to contract the disease, we made sure an SS guard shared in our discomfort. One guard had a favorite name for all of us in prison garb. With sheer pleasure, he addressed us as *du elender hund* (you miserable dog). When the days were warm, he had the habit of taking off his cap and putting it down. That was the sign for us to start gathering lice. Nonchalantly, we would walk by the SS cap and drop in a good number of our animal friends.

The count of corpses increased rapidly as the disease spread. Longtime friends wouldn't show up for morning roll call. In a few weeks, half of the eighty men I worked with were dead.Who would go next? Prisoners overcome by the illness had a choice: keep going until they dropped dead, or report sick. Those who reported to sick bay were stripped of clothing, their heads were shaved, and they were ordered to lie on the concrete floor and wait for death.

I chose the latter option. When fever finally wore down all my resistance, I joined the file of the damned. I stood in line with other miserable men and hardly a word was spoken. There was no more hope. The end had come. Even our underground organization had no power to help.

When I faced der *Herr Artz* (Sir Doctor), he didn't even look up from the notebook on his desk. He allowed me to say a few words, then handed me an aspirin tablet and told me to go next door to an adjacent cell. Then he yelled, *"Der nächste!"* (next one).

Next door I was ordered to strip and was given an old striped shirt, the garment in which I was meant to die. Another prisoner, often called "the can opener," relieved me of all my hair in a few sure strokes. All the while I listened to the refrain from next door: "Der nächste . . . Der nächste . . . Der nächste."

The following day I lost consciousness. Oblivion overcame me for three weeks.

Recollections of bygone days raced through my mind incredibly fast, but the scenes were vivid and clear, and I knew they were true. All the pieces of the puzzle were there, neatly forming a picture of wasted life. There I lay, dying among men of different nationalities. This was the end of the road. My body was only twenty-one years old and was wasted by disease, neglect, and hunger. I weighed a mere seventy pounds!

Yet my spirit groped in the dark to understand spiritual truth—and this probably kept me alive. I knew with certainty there was a life coming that was entirely different from the one I had so far lived in this body. What hypocrisy a lot of my life had been. What ugliness! What a facade I had often put up. Then I prayed again, "Lord, let me live some more. Oh, God, give me another chance, and I promise to serve You when I come out of here."

I had not the slightest notion how I could possibly serve God. I didn't know Him on a personal basis. But whatever I prayed to God in those moments of despair were indeed the deepest desires of my heart. I meant every word with all there was left of me.

For days the mortar shells had exploded nearer and nearer. A high-pitched sound announced the imminent arrival of a shell seconds ahead of the time it struck, and after the ear-splitting explosion came the sound of debris flying in all directions.

Our camp was caught between two warring armies, the

Third American Army of General George S. Patton to the west, and the retreating German army to the east. The noise of their bombardment was terrifying. We were weak and vulnerable. At every explosion we cringed and pulled our arms over our faces—our only defense.

April 10, 1945. Strangely enough, there had been no mortar fire, no flying shrapnel all morning. An eerie silence hung over the concentration camp at Siegburg.

Suddenly a blood-curdling scream shook us out of our reverie, an intense cry coming from someone who seemed extremely happy. A shrill shriek followed, then another, and yet another. The screams began at a part of the building where prisoners could look over the eighteen-foot-high wall. One observer had seen the most beautiful sight any prisoner could expect to witness. His unbelieving eyes were attracted to a large number of American army tanks advancing in the distance. Between the tanks he saw soldiers coming, rifles in hand and ready to fire. He could not suppress that victorious, nearly inhuman scream. Others followed suit, for all of us knew instinctively that our liberator was at the door. Every man who could still shout, howl, yell, shriek, or simply whisper, opened his mouth and let go. It was the sound of ecstasy, the uncontrolled joy of human beasts who smelled freedom. Everyone who lay near any moveable object picked it up, and while still yelling with exuberant joy, banged the object against the walls, on the floor, or against the doors.

An exhilarating sensation began at the top of my head and rippled over my body like giant goose bumps, and an extraordinary stimulation overwhelmed me. The Americans had come! Our liberators were here! We're FREE . . . FREE . . . FREE AT LAST!

Since that moment I have been convinced to the depths of my soul that those who never have been slaves have never really tasted freedom.

At first there seemed to be hardly any resistance from the retreating German troops. But as the first American tanks came closer to the gate, the distant German artillery responded with a dreadful bombardment. We lay very still—happy that the Americans had come, but fearful that a German shell would blow us to bits.

An inmate came to tell us that the camp director had sent two prisoners to the American army with a message of surrender, and that the Americans were actually at the gate. Ever so slowly the sounds of the German artillery came from farther away and we judged that they were in full retreat.

We didn't see any of our liberators for a couple of days. Word spread that they had found the situation in the camp so appalling and the survivors so contaminated with disease that no American GI was allowed inside. They had encountered a place where a thousand men were diseased and many dying, mostly from typhoid. Only about a hundred prisoners could stand up on their own power.

Two days after our liberation, I saw my first American soldier. He was a young man with red hair, a member of an American Red Cross unit. With notebook and pencil in hand, he walked slowly through the rows of sick prisoners, taking inventory of the new liabilities of the American army. Hardly any of us could speak English, so we couldn't bother him with questions. The only information I was able to extract from him was that he was from Boston. But seeing him was a fantastic assurance. We knew that the Americans were finally in control.

Every day the food improved a little, which was a blessing in disguise. Our stomachs were not able to support any sudden increase in calories.

To my utter grief one of my best friends died seven days after liberation. We had been close friends for two years. No amount of medical help could revive the sixty-pound skeleton. Part of his stomach had disintegrated and during his last days he was only able to whisper a few hoarse words. For him and many others, liberation came too late.

In contrast, my health improved by leaps and bounds, and a zest for life again took hold of me.

The American occupation forces wouldn't let many ex-prisoners through the gate, partly for fear of spreading diseases, partly because they wanted to regulate the flow of the millions of former prisoners out of Germany. After four weeks, however, a number of us had sufficiently recovered and a transport column was organized to take us to a displaced persons camp. There everyone was properly identified and the repatriation process began.

Two months after liberation, I set foot on Dutch soil again, still weak but feeling considerably better. Dutch soldiers armed with tommy guns received the contingent of ex-prisoners and put us up in a school for the night. All exits were guarded by zealous volunteers of the new Dutch army. I was so disgusted to have to look into the muzzle of a gun again that I climbed over the gate that surrounded the school.

One of the soldiers threatened me with an automatic rifle, but I told him decidedly, "I've been a prisoner long enough. If you want to shoot me, go ahead." Intimidated, the soldier slowly lowered the muzzle of the rifle and watched me climb on over the gate.

From that border town in southern Holland, I hitchhiked to the west in Canadian army trucks to my home village of Monster.

My reception at home was overwhelming. However, the joy of my homecoming was dampened because of the many other war victims who had not returned and never would.

As I tried to relate my experiences to my family, I found myself unable to share the painful impressions and horrors of the last four years. Words were not adequate to express the emotions that haunted me.

To my amazement I found that my ex-communist friend had also survived. In spite of his self-imposed diet, he had come through. He had been one of the first to arrive in his own country. With a happy melody in his heart, he walked up to the street where his wife and two children lived—and saw the two men whose names he had divulged to the SS. They stood in front of his house, and he was frightened. What were they up to? Had they come to square with him for reporting them?

The moment the two recognized him, they overwhelmed him with warm greetings, gestures he surely had not expected from them. Had the SS not arrested them?

No! The SS had been convinced that his fourth and true story was just as false as his three previous ones. The God in whom he had put his trust had not let him down. He was the first man I ever met who had trusted God implicitly, and he had fared better than most of us with all our devious ways.

The ex-communist's experience made me think. However, there was quite a difference in his simple faith and my intellectual acceptance of the existence of a God, or my subscribing to some articles of faith. It was not that I doubted this God; in fact, I was very sure of an Almighty Being, because I had met Him when I lay so near death in Siegburg. But I did not know Him on a personal basis. I was dead spiritually.

I had begun reading the Bible in which my ex-communist friend had had such an intense interest. The sad part was that I wasn't equally gripped with the content. Besides the stories about the life of Jesus, I understood little of what I read.

What about the promise, the vow I had made that I would serve God forever if He would see me through? I had surely meant every syllable but had no idea how to go about it. How can one serve God without knowing or loving Him?

Chapter Two

A NEW LIFE BECKONS

If this was a liberated country, it had little attraction for me. Not that I was ungrateful, far from it, but civilized life in post-war Holland had many complications.

There was hardly any work, no real chance to get ahead, and the bureaucracy strangled and stifled any ideas a young man might have. The country was crowded, dull, void of real individual freedom. Everything had changed. Holland no longer seemed like home.

In reality *I* had changed. My spirit was restless. All the dreadful memories of the past four years pursued me relentlessly. I made a long list of the many men I had known who had lost their lives; I could still see each of their sad faces.

When picking berries in our garden, I would carefully survey my immediate surroundings to make sure there was no danger. Life in the camps had trained me to be suspicious.

Memories were too fresh and vivid. How I longed to get away from Holland, with all its disappointments. How I longed to leave behind all those greedy, selfish people, and start anew somewhere else. Having lived for years in close quarters with other prisoners, I had often experienced a bond of camaraderie not so apparent in this free society.

My eyes were more open to the faults of others. Many of the prisoners I had known were less selfish than the residents of this Free World.

Several months after liberation I developed heart trouble. The doctor's verdict was that through the sustained misery my heart was enlarged. I was ordered to rest. No sunshine, no coffee, no work, no excitement, absolutely nothing, just rest. That gave me time to think. I wanted to get away from Europe, its evils, and my war memories. I wanted to make a new start in another country far away. The more I thought about it, the more my yearning grew.

When I had sufficiently recuperated, a bold plan took shape in my mind. I would begin a new life in South Africa.

Why South Africa and not Australia or America? For two simple reasons: First, to reach South Africa I had to cross only one sea, the Mediterranean. Except for that one sea, I could walk to South Africa. Emigrating to any other country worth emigrating to meant passage by ship, which I could not afford.

Secondly, I had met a Dutchman from South Africa who had served in the Dutch Free Forces, and he greatly encouraged me to join him in South Africa. So, I had a contact there.

In my mind's eye, I could see the sunny shores of that far-away country. But the list of difficulties that lay ahead did not speak in my favor. Though the Dutch government had issued a passport in my name, it was impossible just after the war to obtain visas or special permits for the fifteen countries I had to pass through. I had no money to facilitate this tremendous undertaking, nor did I have a permanent resident permit for South Africa.

To my credit were some highly questionable qualifications: a determination to leave the ugly past behind; and high hopes that the government of South Africa would allow me to enter the country on the sheer merits of my exploits. The only other means at my disposal were my two feet, hitching an occasional ride, and a willingness to work wherever I could.

When I revealed my plans to my parents, my father objected.

"Do you realize the problems you will have to face?"

"Nothing that lies ahead can be worse than what I've been through the last four years," I replied with earnestness.

With this my father agreed.

I made a backpack, bought a small aluminum pan, got some clothes together, and a New Testament. I packed everything and was ready to leave the old country for good.

Dad offered me my first ride into the unknown. We spoke few words as he drove me from our village to The Hague, ten

miles away. As he dropped me off on a bridge on the main highway going south, he said his farewell.

"Well, son, I wish you all the best."

Then he turned the car around and disappeared up the road.
Oh, yes, he meant those words, but we Dutch were taught from
early youth to control our emotions.

Just after the war, there were few cars on the road, but most
drivers showed a willingness to help a heavily-packed stranger.
Often I spent nights in freight trains, or barns, or under the open
sky. Life was wonderful and free. Not even the Mediterranean
was a major obstacle. An understanding captain of a small
coaster didn't mind smuggling human cargo to North Africa for
a good cause.

As the coastline of France disappeared beyond the horizon,
I took a last look at the continent where I had lost the best years
of my youth, and then shouted in German, because it expressed
my feelings best, "Europe, I hope I never see you again!"

The little coaster needed two-and-a-half days of plowing
through the azure blue waters of the Mediterranean to arrive at
Bone, a port in Algeria, North Africa. From then on the challenges came in twos and threes. Strange Arab customs, no
money, the French military police, malaria, no visas, sunstroke,
jail, all tried to wedge into my determination to forge ahead. But
I was a stubborn man.

Trying to reach Egypt and follow the Nile upstream, I had
to pass through Tunisia. After entering the country illegally, I
was caught and deported to Algeria. A young Frenchman, a sur-
vivor of Dachau, joined me and together we made our way to
Morocco, hoping to reach the Atlantic at Casablanca and from
there find a way south. We were refused permission to enter
Morocco and the Frenchman gave up. But not this stubborn
Dutchman! I remained convinced that somewhere there must be
a loophole in this solid wall of officialdom.

I spent little time praying and reading my New Testament. I
still marveled at the God who had been so real in the lowest and
neediest moments of my life. But everyday problems and neces-
sities made serving this God seem somehow remote.

Chapter Three

THE DESERT RAT

For a year I lived a primitive life in tents in the rugged interior of Algeria. A French construction company working on a huge pipeline offered me a job as a foreman. Run-down and sick with malaria, I accepted; I didn't feel like traveling. Working with an Arab crew and saving a few francs from each payday, I remained always on the lookout for an opportunity to cross the giant continent of Africa.

Unexpectedly, at the edge of the enormous Sahara, the green light went on. Sitting in an Arab cafe, enjoying sweet tea in the oasis Colomb-Bechar, I saw an item in the local newspaper:

A convoy of three trucks with twenty-two Englishmen as passengers has passed through Oran on its way to Algiers. This is another group of emigrants heading for South Africa and they are trying to cover the distance from here by truck.

Mr. C., one of the emigrants, told our correspondent that this group intends to spend some weeks in Algiers to stock the necessary supplies and to secure the needed documents before they are able to undertake the most difficult crossing in the world, the Sahara.

The organizers of this convoy are planning to follow the track over the Hoggar mountains, and . . .

My eyes flew over the rest of the article as I realized that this was the chance I had been waiting for. Again I read it, then spelled it out word for word to make certain I understood.

A ramshackle train which kept communications open

between Oran on the Mediterranean and Colomb-Bechar in the south of Algeria had brought me here. Colomb-Bechar was one of the last outposts of civilization, but at the same time the entire area was military country where the French Foreign Legion ruled with an iron hand and where I was not allowed to be without a special permit.

I had arrived here with all my savings, about 30,000 francs, the equivalent of $150. Besides this small sum of money, nothing had changed for the better. I still had a driving obsession to reach South Africa at all costs. So far, however, I had not been able to proceed beyond Colomb-Bechar. The road farther south was little more than marks left by car tires in the sand.

In the course of loafing around the village, I had discovered that there was a company fittingly called the "Trans Sahara Company," which held a monopoly on transporting passengers through the desert. But the cost was much more than I could afford, and I didn't have permission to cross military territory.

I walked around for days and gazed at the enormous rocky plains south of the oasis. This part of the Sahara was aptly called the "Stone Desert." Though a few glaring white sand dunes showed here and there, the prevailing color was the gray-black of billions of rocks.

It was at that crucial moment that I had bought the newspaper which told about the English expedition. The few lines worked like magic. Suddenly I knew what I had to do and it excited and sharpened my senses. With the paper still in hand, I started planning how to offer my services to these Englishmen—what I should say, and how to improve my poor English in such a short time. That very day I started the six hundred miles back to Algiers, in search of these fast-moving emigrants.

A few days later I arrived in the Paris of North Africa, as Algiers is often called. Searching for half a day, I discovered a Dodge truck with English number plates parked in front of the British consulate. *Desert Rat* was painted on the hood. The sight of the truck quickened my blood. The decisive moment was there; the course of the next quarter of an hour would be of tremendous importance to my future.

There were six people in the truck, two women and four men. A tall blond fellow towering above the others gave orders in English.

"Are you the people going to South Africa?" I asked in my school English. No one answered and the eyes of all six stared at me.

I began reeling off English phrases I'd learned by heart. I told them I was a Dutchman on my way to South Africa, and that I had been trying for a year to overcome the various difficulties to reaching that country.

When I finished, they remained quiet for a few moments, then the older of the women leaned forward and said, "You did say that you're Dutch, didn't you?"

"Yes, ma'am."

"Then you should talk Dutch with my husband here. His mother was Dutch, and he still speaks the language."

"Well, in a way," the tall man interrupted from under a large red mustache. "I was born in South Africa. My father was English, my mother Dutch, so I speak both." He was speaking in Afrikaans, the South African adaptation of Holland Dutch.

"I'm the leader of this outfit," he said. "Now tell your story again more slowly so that I can understand you."

Once more I related briefly the reason for my visit. Then I asked, "Do you think there is a chance you could take me down to South Africa, sir?"

I was over-anxious for an answer.

"Take it easy," the tall man said. "Take it easy. Don't be in such a hurry. Tell me, would you be able to pay something if we decide to take you along? As you know, traveling costs money."

"I've saved up a little money," I said, eager to show my good will. Afraid of losing the opportunity, I added, "I can give you thirty thousand francs right now."

"Would you be prepared to work?" he asked, ignoring my offer of money.

"Sure," I said with conviction, "whatever you want."

"I might need someone to help with the cooking," he said, "and once in a while I can use a man to drive one of my trucks."

"Of course I can do that," I said, "and perhaps you could

use the services of an interpreter. I speak fluent French and some Arabic, and . . ."

"That's quite all right," he cut me off. "Give me some time to think about it and then I'd like to get my friends' views about taking on another passenger. This is not a matter I can decide at a moment's notice. But tomorrow at the same time we'll be back here on this spot. Then I'll let you know whether you can come along with us to South Africa."

I was disappointed that I wouldn't know till next morning, but could understand their wanting to talk it over. All day I walked around in a dream, wondering about the *Desert Rat* and her silent company.

"If I could only get into that truck," I kept thinking anxiously, "then the rest of my trip through Africa would be a picnic."

Long before ten the next morning, I was waiting in front of the British consulate. When the truck still hadn't shown up at eleven, I started giving up hope. Just when I was on the point of leaving, the *Desert Rat* whizzed around the corner and stopped in front of me.

"Get in the truck, Dutchy," someone shouted at me. "Everything is okay."

Overjoyed, I jumped in the back and sat among the silent Englishmen. The driver continued his course down the road and turned into one of the side streets.

After five minutes we stopped in front of a bar and everyone got out. When we were seated on stools at the bar with cognacs in front of us, I was officially presented to the rest of the group.

Castor, the tall leader, presented me first to his wife, Ann, and stepdaughter, Dolly. Then I shook hands with the males, James, Dan, and Dick. We emptied the glasses and they were filled again. The Englishmen got into a conversation of their own, while Castor took me aside to reveal some of his plans for the trip.

He said the convoy contained three trucks, and the emigrants in the two other vehicles had stayed behind in camp. Castor and his three friends arranged the various business deals for the entire party. They were trying to get a transit visa for the Sahara, and to organize the food supply for the crossing. The convoy had been on its way from England for more than two months, and everyone was eager for the next adventure, crossing the largest desert in the world.

His convincing way of explaining the details gave me great confidence in the undertaking.

After absorbing more brandy, the other Englishmen came out of their shells and seemed to accept me. I began to feel at ease. We spent the rest of the afternoon celebrating in several bars.

After dark we climbed into the truck and zigzagged through the streets in the same way the Englishmen had walked from the last bar to the truck. I sat next to Castor, who hung onto the wheel for dear life. More to himself than to anyone else, he hummed the same song again and again. "Rolling home . . . rolling home . . . by the light of the silvery moon . . ."

Nearing camp, he changed into a more serious mood and said to me, "If the other people in the camp don't talk to you, don't worry, pal. You see, they aren't the friendliest type; but you've got nothing to do with them. Just remember, I am the big boss, the captain, the leader, and so I am their leader, too."

Half drunk as he was, one couldn't expect the most reasonable conversation.

We turned off the road at the top of a hill and sailed through some magnificent fir trees to where the other trucks were parked. On the hood of one was printed *Southern Cross*, and on the other glittered the letters *Cape of Good Hope*. This was the other two-thirds of the convoy. Most of the men and women sat around a campfire on which they were preparing dinner.

When we stopped our truck and approached the others on foot, everyone shut his mouth. No one greeted anyone. Though I knew the English were a rather surly people, this silence seemed unnatural. Why wouldn't these people talk to each other? They were on a large-scale venture together and had known each other for months.

"Ladies and gentlemen," Castor yelled louder than necessary. When everyone looked at him, he said, "Tonight at eight we'll have a meeting in the white tent. Then we can talk matters over and perhaps come to an agreement."

As we walked slowly back to the *Desert Rat*, he remarked to me, "Did you notice that these people are looking for trouble, Dutchy? I know they prefer someone else to be their leader; they don't like the way I've organized this crossing. They've paid the fare, but I have to remind them once and for all that I will stay in charge. Don't you forget that either, Dutchy; there is only one leader, and that's me, and me alone!"

A few minutes before eight o'clock I entered the white tent. Most of the others were already present. Some sat on empty cases, others on the floor, all neatly arranged in a circle against the canvas.

Castor waited till all twenty-three emigrants were seated and then started his speech. It was soon obvious that most of the others resented his leadership. After a heated discussion it was decided to vote for a second in command.

The moment the assistant was chosen, the atmosphere seemed less tense, and the next item on the agenda was discussed. Castor had promised mosquito netting which he had not provided. The group complained there was not enough food and that it was of poor quality. In short, all possible complaints were being aired.

I didn't know whether or not the accusations were true, but the language was far from diplomatic. The men shouted and swore, calling Castor a "dirty colonial." Castor shrugged his shoulders and in turn called them liars.

Suddenly there was a loud curse and the hurricane lamp came down with a crash, throwing the tent into pitch darkness. Someone had deliberately knocked the lamp down and was now flailing away with his fists. In a few seconds the meeting had become a howling gang fight. Women screamed and cried. Men cursed and threw punches. The large tent sagged and I crept on all fours out of the mess, disappointed with Castor and his British friends.

Half an hour later life in camp had returned to normal. I lay down on the front seat of the *Desert Rat* and tried to sleep. The stillness of the night hung in the big trees around me, but disquieting thoughts crisscrossed my mind. During this first day with the convoy, I had already lost nearly all confidence in the success of the venture. It was too late to turn back, however—I had given up my hard-earned cash.

My new travel companions were like a pack of wild dogs. Why? Why was the group so divided? Every member had paid for the entire trip and for that reason alone Castor had to take all of us to South Africa. All of us had signed some sort of contract with him.

And surely there was plenty of money. Castor had shown me a letter of credit worth the fantastic amount of 2,500 pounds. With such capital behind us the trip to South Africa should be a pleasure cruise all the way. So why all this distrust and suspicion?

Not one of the sixteen emigrants around the campfire wanted to have anything to do with Castor or the five others who had picked me up in town that morning. Something must have grown between the two groups, something I still knew nothing about.

I had been a member of the convoy for about ten days and was getting accustomed to life with the British, I thought. Every morning Castor took us, the "privileged six," to town. We spent most of our time in bars, mainly to be away from the unpleasant atmosphere among the other sixteen in the camp.

Nothing much was said about our imminent departure, but impatience grew within me and I asked Castor when he thought we'd be leaving. He said, "We have to wait until we get permits to cross the desert. The Algerian government requires a certain amount of money from us for security purposes. In case we get stuck in the Sahara, the French want to be able to rescue us with our own money. I am now in the process of getting these permits . . . without paying this security money. Do you understand?"

When I inquired further, Castor only looked at me with penetrating eyes and answered in an irritated voice, "Just leave the arrangements to me, Dutchy. I've got enough brains up here. Above all, don't forget that I am the leader and I know what I'm doing. All I want you to do is obey!"

Trusting someone blindly didn't come easy to me; in the Nazi death camps I had learned to be suspicious. But I had given Castor my down payment and was determined to stick it out. Turning back never entered my mind. I was running from Europe; I wanted to put as much distance as possible between myself and all those bad memories.

One evening just after dark Castor was again attacked by his opponents. They threatened to shoot him if he didn't straighten out their difficulties. Castor decided the time had come to get rid of the sixteen Englishmen who, he said, were double-crossing him. The morning after the attack he spoke softly to me, "Dutchy, these people will kill me when we reach the Sahara. I'm going to avoid that; I'm going to get a lawyer and leave these backbiters behind lawfully. Come along with me as my interpreter."

Soon we arrived at a prestigious-looking building in downtown Algiers. On the nameplate were the engraved letters: M. J. RASSENY—AVOCAT. When I knocked at the door on the second floor, a muffled voice answered, "Entrez!"

Behind a heavy mahogany desk sat a middle-aged man. His hair was gray at the temples, giving him an aristocratic appearance.

After introducing ourselves, Castor started to explain his difficulties with the other members of the convoy. I translated his words into French for Rasseny.

Listening carefully to Castor's story, the lawyer pursed his lips and mused, "So it is your intention to leave the sixteen emigrants here in Algiers because you are afraid you will be murdered in the Sahara?"

"I have studied to be a lawyer," Castor continued without directly answering the question, "and I know the tricks of this trade. That is why, before I left England, I had a contract made up with all the people who would undertake this trip with me. Each emigrant paid me three hundred pounds for the fare, for which I gave him a contract assuring him safe passage to South Africa.

"But by way of precaution, I had some clauses added to the contract to cover myself, just in case of emergency. Now that

28

some of these fellow travelers have made an attempt on my life, they have forced me to make use of one of these clauses."

He took a typewritten sheet of paper out of his khaki coat pocket and handed it to the lawyer. "This is the clause I want to make use of," Castor explained, indicating a paragraph near the bottom of the page. "I assure you, these few lines will serve my purpose." He hesitated a moment, then read:

In the event that an amount of money has to be paid for eventual visas, or if any cash is to be deposited as a guarantee or security before the emigrant is allowed to cross any country, then the traveler himself will be responsible for the required amount and not the leader of the expedition.

Castor looked up with a gleam in his eyes, but the lawyer kept quiet. Castor continued, "This is the part which entitles me legally to part company with the sixteen insurgents. As you probably know, Monsieur Rasseny, every person who wishes to cross the Sahara must deposit an amount of cash, called security money, with the Algerian government. This money is reimbursed as soon as the traveler reaches the other side of the desert without the help of authorities. The amount requested is rather high. You can understand that under the circumstances I can't take the risk of paying the security money for these people—only to be buried by them somewhere in the sands of the Sahara.

"I know that not one of the sixteen has much cash, and each will have to pay this sum himself, according to our mutual contract. They are in no position to pay, so they will not be able to live up to our agreement. Therefore, I can leave them behind without doing injustice to any of them. What do you think, Monsieur Rasseny? Do you have to take this matter to court?"

The lawyer didn't answer immediately. Softly he hit the back of his pen on his desk and stared at the faded green blotting paper in front of him. It was obvious that he was considering certain aspects of the case that Castor might not have thought of.

Finally he said, pronouncing each word carefully, "It is my

profession to give you advice, Messieurs, but your case puts me in a difficult position. According to this stipulation in your contract, you are on the safe side and I'm certain that we would win a court case; but there are two sides to every coin, and the other side is very ugly.

"Let us suppose we win this case and you leave these people behind. They are in a foreign country; they don't speak the language; and as you were saying, they have no funds whatsoever. Who is going to put up with them? The local authorities, of course. Because you disagree with two-thirds of your party, the taxpayer will have to pay the expenses incurred. Are you sure that this dispute cannot be settled out of court and in a friendlier manner? For example, we could convene all members of the convoy and discuss the problems together to find a solution. In any case, I feel it is worth trying."

When I translated this legal advice to Castor, a dangerous light flickered in his eyes. Putting a little too much emphasis in his words, he replied, "I have approached you, Monsieur Rasseny, to ask your advice with regard to a contract. I don't require any help in my personal affairs. I wish to leave these sixteen hoodlums behind and believe that I have a legal right to do so. I would like you to start proceedings as soon as you possibly can, because the rest of us are anxious to continue the trip to South Africa."

"Do the six others have enough money to pay the required security fee?" the lawyer asked.

"No, they don't have that kind of money, either," Castor replied, "One can leave England with no more than five pounds sterling in cash and a small amount in traveler's checks. But I will advance these six people the money for the time being."

"What means of payment do you use to settle your financial matters, if you were not allowed to leave England with any money?" the lawyer asked, ignoring Castor's cunning eye.

"I've got a letter of credit for the amount of twenty-five hundred pounds," Castor disclosed, allowing a faint touch of pride in his voice. Caressing his red mustache with the back of his hand, he added, "That's more than enough to get to South Africa, don't you think?"

"In the capacity of your lawyer," Rasseny said, "would you mind if I had a look at that document, Monsieur?"

Slowly Castor extracted the important paper from his inside coat pocket and held it up at a distance from Rasseny. "You see," he said triumphantly, "here it states on the front page: 'Letter of Credit. Available amount £2,500.'"

"I cannot read that far off," the Frenchman protested. "You wouldn't mind if I just had a quick look at this valuable document?" he insisted.

When the lawyer held out his hand, Castor parted reluctantly with the letter. Then Rasseny opened the document and centered his attention on its contents. While studying it, he knit his eyebrows.

After a few silent moments, he closed the pages again and handed Castor his letter of credit. Castor eyed the lawyer suspiciously while *he* looked at Castor, biting his underlip. Then he raised his hand and pointed to the door.

"Get out, Messieurs," he said emphatically. "There is the exit." His tone was superior, as if he were addressing a pair of beggars. Contempt dripped from his voice.

Castor didn't need my translation to understand these French words. He looked paler than usual and nervously turned his letter of credit into a roll.

"I told you to leave!" the lawyer repeated.

Bewildered, I stared at the Frenchman and finally was able to say, "Monsieur l'avocat, what is the matter? What is wrong with this document? I do not understand."

The lawyer looked at me searchingly, and then asked with a jeer in his voice, "Do you really think that this man will be able to guide twenty-three people to South Africa when he has only fifty pounds on his letter of credit? That isn't even enough to cover my fee. It is only too obvious why he prefers to leave most of his people behind."

Suddenly my eyes were opened and I realized that I was involved with a crook who had no conscience. I turned to Castor, who still fiddled with his "important" paper, and began to stutter, "Uh . . . uh . . . according to the lawyer, y-y-you've got only fifty pounds left on your account. Do you th . . ."

"This is not the place to discuss this matter," he interrupted. "Come on, we'd better leave. This man might blow his top any moment."

He turned and strode along the rows of books on the shelves and disappeared through the door. I watched Rasseny and noticed that he followed Castor closely with his eyes. Slowly he shook his head. Then I too hurried from the stuffy room.

Dozens of thoughts ran through my mind. I felt a sudden contempt for the man who, with a smile on his face and a flow of refined words, had taken my hard-earned money. He had accepted my fare knowing he would never be able to take me to South Africa. He only needed my money, not me.

I also realized why there had been conflict among the emigrants. Castor had kept as his friends only those who could still be of some financial use to him. He had dealt arrogantly with the rest, needling them so that they would resist him as commander, giving him a legal excuse to break his contract with them.

In years past I had dealt with the scum of the earth, but this devilish scheme left me dumbfounded. Should I just walk away from this scam, or should I tell the other emigrants about our captain's manipulations and try to get my money back? Perhaps it would be better to strike out on my own again, without money and without papers. No, I decided. The thief had taken my money, and I would try to get out of him whatever I could. That was my right.

"Castor, you conceited gangster," I said, "for the time being I will stick around, whether you like it or not."

He said nothing, and as I loafed along the sidewalks on my way to the garage where the *Desert Rat* was parked, I felt like a rat in a trap.

Chapter Four

IN THE SPIDER'S WEB

At last we were on our way. After three weeks of delay in Algiers, we rolled southward. I sat in the back of the *Desert Rat* on a pile of luggage and noticed how the trees along the road rushed past. I was not excited. Glad to be on the go, yes, but not excited, having lost all confidence in the enterprise.

During our last week in Algiers, the friction between the groups had gone from bad to worse. The sixteen rebels had also hired a lawyer and tried to get Castor into court, and when their efforts appeared to be futile, eight of them appropriated the *Southern Cross* and disappeared during the night. They joined another convoy of Englishmen, also going south. Before they left, they sabotaged the *Cape of Good Hope* and the *Desert Rat*. After inspecting the trucks, Castor concluded that the *Cape of Good Hope* was beyond repair.

The *Desert Rat* was less damaged. Although sand had been poured into the radiator and crankcase, after a thorough cleaning it would run, albeit slowly and without much power.

The sabotage was a relief for Castor. Now he really had a good reason to abandon the rest of the group. We towed the *Cape of Good Hope* to a garage; and after a day of negotiation, a deal was made with the garage owner: He took the useless truck, but instead of paying cash for it, he assumed responsibility and costs for any breakdown during our Sahara crossing.

After this guarantee was forwarded to the Algerian government, we set out on the big adventure, a group of seven in an old army truck.

I was better acquainted with my fellow passengers after the three weeks in Algiers.

James was Castor's right hand. He followed the "boss" like a dog, obeying every command. James apparently was the only person Castor trusted.

Dick, a tall, thin man of about forty, was without a trade or profession and without much spirit. He longed for adventure, but I wasn't sure he would have the spirit to handle it when he found it. He had given his savings to Castor in exchange for a trip that excited his imagination.

Dan had been a grocery clerk, and because of that he was designated our cook. He had little backbone, but he was the most likable fellow of the group, and certainly the most talkative. He had a bank account in both East and West Africa and that made him a preferred risk in Castor's eyes. Because of Dan's financial state, Castor treated him with a little more respect than the rest of us.

Castor's wife, Ann, was seventeen years older than her husband. She was nice to us without exception, and she cared more for her husband than he cared for her. As far as I could discover, she had put up most of the money for the journey.

Ann's daughter, Dolly, had been born in Ann's previous marriage. Why she had come on this dusty trip to South Africa, no one knew.

Big drops of water hit the canvas over our heads. The wooden water barrel behind us was leaking and the drinking water was oozing through my clothes. Dick spread out in all his glory on a pile of luggage. He had hidden his long face in a grubby, multi-colored blanket. Only his unkempt hair stuck up from between the folds.

James had crept among the food cases. His head tilted forward and his chin rested on his chest. He snored loudly, proving he was either sleeping or overcome with liquor.

Castor's long feet hung over me like a menacing sword. Our leader had climbed on top of the luggage to sober up. The left side of his jacket swung over the water barrel and out of his pocket peeked the neck of a half-empty bottle of cognac.

Dan drove. We planned to travel day and night to make up for the three weeks we had lost in Algiers. Castor also changed the original plan of going directly south from Algiers.

I suspected he was afraid of meeting our former companions, who might be lying in wait for us somewhere ahead. His pretense was that he wanted to go to Oran first to get another permit for gas.

From Oran we would go straight south: first to Colomb-Bechar; next the crossing of the *Tanezrouft*, the "Land of Thirst"; then on to the shores of the Niger, the enormous river in French West Africa. From there, plans were to follow the thousand-mile dirt road leading to Kano in Nigeria.

The evening we left, Castor solemnly announced this new itinerary. Wisely, he didn't mention his lack of money. He knew that somewhere along the long stretch of road we would run out of gas, or out of food, or both. In the last week, he had gone to the bank only once. He had made sure no one was near when he opened his letter of credit and pocketed the money.

He gave Dan three pounds to buy food for a couple of days. Otherwise, we didn't see any of the cash. Castor wasted it in various bars. What he intended to do with us, without food or gas in the middle of the Sahara, remained a mystery; but he appeared to be without worry.

A dimly lighted gas station on the side of the road indicated there was still an attendant to serve us. We didn't need gas; we only needed water, and plenty of it.

In spite of the heavy rain, the needle of our temperature gauge pointed persistently to the boiling point, so at every gas station we stopped to change the water. Each time the radiator was drained the water came out a dirty brown, due to the sand and mud in the radiator. We also had to drain and refill the crankcase at each stop.

Soaking wet, we took our places on the luggage again and moved on at a snail's pace. The night was pitch dark. Not a single light brightened the long road. Incessantly the rain beat on the heavy canvas above us, its monotonous melody reminding me of the plaintive music of the Arabs.

A couple of nights later, we tried to pass the night in a miserable, windswept camp on the side of the road. Castor knew nothing of choosing campsites—or he didn't care. Like a puppy, I lay rolled up in a little hole I had dug in the sand. Through the leafless bushes overhead came the twinkling of a hundred thousand stars. A cool wind chased dead leaves across the plain.

In the distance I watched a long file of vehicles creeping along the winding road like a brightly-lighted caterpillar. As the trucks drew nearer, I saw that it was an army unit on the move. Heavy-caliber guns were being pulled by large six-wheelers, and most of the trucks were loaded with soldiers armed to the teeth. This was a unit of the *Legion Etrangere*, the French Foreign Legion. Sidi-Bel-Abbes, headquarters of this famed international army, was only a couple of miles away.

Enviously I watched the new trucks as they passed along the road like large shadows. Judging by the fading stars, it must have been about five o'clock in the morning.

Suddenly one of the trucks slid off the road and came to a halt against a pile of stones. The legionnaires jumped out and scurried around the truck like ants. Three halftracks stopped and picked up the stranded troops, leaving the truck with two men to watch her.

When the truck column had disappeared, I got up and walked toward the soldiers left on guard, who had retreated to the warmth of the truck cabin.

"Engine trouble?" I asked.

"No brakes, that's all," the driver answered, yawning.

"They'll send a tow truck up from Sidi-Bel-Abbes," the assistant said.

"What are you doing on the road in the middle of the night?" I inquired.

"I could ask the same of you," the driver replied, not in the best of humor, "but if you insist on knowing, we're on maneuvers. What are you guys doing here? Couldn't you find a better camping site?"

Sheltered on one side of the Legion truck, I shared the painful story of the whims of the *Desert Rat*. I told them how the truck had been sabotaged, about the many times we had drained the oil and water, and about the various overhauls—after all of which our truck still had no power.

"We can check it out," the driver said. "Wait until it's a little lighter."

Two hours later, all of us were bent over the engine of the *Desert Rat*. The soldiers, an Italian and a Spaniard, checked the compression, overhauled the carburetor, stripped the distributor, yet there was no improvement. They were nonplused.

"I'd go to the central depot of the Legion, if I were you," said the Italian. "They'll fix that wagon of yours for nothing."

"You must be kidding," I said. "Do you mean it wouldn't cost us a centime?"

"Not a penny," he answered. "The Legion will take care of you. It's kind of tricky to get in, but once inside the walls, you've got it made."

Hearing about repairs at no cost made Castor perk up and take control. Stroking his mustache, a sign of his being sober and thinking, he said, "Maybe we'll get rid of our Jonah after all." After a few moments, he added, "Dutchy, you are the most suitable person to get us inside those barracks. Let's be on our way."

We drove slowly into Sidi-Bel-Abbes. At the gate of the Legion headquarters I got off. Two sentries guarded the entrance like statues. I approached the first and asked him which officer we should see about truck repairs. He didn't answer, but continued to look straight ahead, not moving a muscle. I then addressed the second guard, with the same result.

Walking along the wall I reached the next gate, where two more soldiers stood stiff-backed. Again I gave my little speech and studied the legionnaire. He didn't blink when spoken to, but kept his gaze fixed on outer space. However, he did answer me. I could just see his lips move, and his reply was barely audible.

"You'll have to ask one of the officers yourself," he said. Motionless, he looked straight through me.

"What officer?" I asked. "What's his name?"

"Just try some of the officers who go in and out of this gate. One of them will tell you what to do."

Hearing footsteps approaching, the sentry shut up. Three

officers walked past. One looked at us suspiciously, but marched on without a word. When they were far enough away that they couldn't hear us, I continued the conversation.

"Are you sure they repair private trucks in the workshop?"

"Positive."

"Where are you from?"

"Belgium."

"Been in the Legion a long time?"

"Almost two years."

"You like it?"

"It's all right."

"Are they rough on you guys?"

"It all depends. It's a matter of adapting yourself. It's your tough luck if you don't."

Two lieutenants walked out the gate and I chanced, "Messieurs, pardonnez-moi. Is there a possibility of our truck being repaired at the central depot?"

The officers stopped and I explained in a few words the deficiencies of the *Desert Rat*.

"You should see Captain Bralan," one of the officers suggested. "Just tell him Lieutenant de Boulonge sent you." Then, addressing the Belgian guard, "Let this man through. He's got to see Captain Bralan."

Walking through the gate of the Foreign Legion, I was sure that half the battle was won. The area swarmed with legionnaires. They wore the same uniform as the French army; only their caps were different. Each recruit sported a white *kepi*—a military cap with black visor.

When I found Captain Bralan, he listened politely as I recited our troubles.

"It is correct that private trucks are repaired here occasionally," he said, "but I do not have the authority to let you in the depot. You'll have to see Colonel Hussard."

An hour went by and I couldn't locate Colonel Hussard, but I spoke to another ten officers, ranging from a lieutenant to a commander. Not one wanted to take the risk of permitting us to bring our truck within the walls. All were experts at passing the buck. Up and down the ranks it went.

When I was ready to give up, a soldier took me to a lieutenant who was in charge of the Legion's repair shop. Lieutenant Cressant was a short, stocky man who had sympathy for any truck with mechanical shortcomings. Hearing that I had talked with at least ten of his colleagues, he grinned and said, "Bring that truck inside. We'll see what we can do!"

A few minutes later the *Desert Rat* moved triumphantly through the barracks gate. Three mechanics were called and told to give the engine a thorough check. All three spoke German. The German element was usually above sixty percent in the Legion. No one could guess how many war criminals were among these soldiers of fortune. Having taken refuge in the battalions of the Legion, they knew that they would be safe for the next five years. Then the grateful French republic would offer them French citizenship for their faithful service.

Englishmen and Americans were few in this international army, though some army deserters had joined. There were many Spaniards and Italians. The percentages of nationals in the Legion varied along with the political and economic fortunes of European countries. At that moment, it was a good place for Germans.

Many had joined for other reasons—criminals fleeing justice, adventurers, drunks, and desperadoes. All came to Sidi-Bel-Abbes to find in the Legion a haven, a refuge in time of distress. Recruits could use fake names, falsify their dates of birth and even their nationality. In the annals of the Legion they were simply men known by numbers. Yet out of these diverse elements, France had forged an extremely well-disciplined army.

Looking around in the cradle of France's most gallant fighting force, I felt a tap on my shoulder. I turned to see a blond soldier, who asked in Dutch, "Someone told me you're from Holland. Is that right?"

"Yes," I replied, "that's correct."

He offered his hand. "Piet de Groot is my name."

"André Vandenberg is mine." We looked at each other for a few moments, then I broke the silence.

"How did you get here?" I asked, not expecting even a half-truth in answer.

But he surprised me.

"I'm running from the Dutch government."

"You were with the SS?"

"No, that's not the case," he said. "When I was called for military duty in Holland, I ran. If I ever get caught, it will cost me a few years in the cage. I was a stupid fool. I should have let them lock me up. I probably would have gotten out with a general amnesty. Here I'll be tied up for five years, and when I go home the police will still arrest me."

"You talk as if you're sorry you signed up. How do they treat you?"

"I can't complain. I've got a special assignment."

"Doing what?"

"Better change the subject, man."

"Come on! Don't be ridiculous. I'm no part of your Legion."

"I bring deserters back."

"You bring them back where?"

"Back here to Sidi-Bel-Abbes."

"And then what happens?"

"They're beaten up."

"What happens after the beatings?"

"If they survive, they go to the Sahara, to one of the penal settlements. Ever heard of *casser les caillous?*"

"Sure enough," I said. "It's breaking up rocks with sledge hammers in the stone desert."

"Exactly. That's where they end up, chopping big boulders into small pieces, usually on their bare feet."

"Aren't they sentenced to a certain time?"

"Yes. Some do two years at hard labor, others three. The bad part is that the time they spend breaking rocks is not counted as part of their five years of service."

"What a waste of time. Do they go back to the Legion when they have served their sentences?"

"If they survive . . ." Piet had walked back with me to the workshop.

From the opposite direction, a colonel approached. The moment he noticed us around the truck, he began to curse loudly. Piet ran off like a rabbit, white kepi in hand. The waves of abuse were not meant for him. In between the streams of blasphemy, I caught a few words: "Out with your junk . . . within five minutes . . . thought you could bypass me . . . you . . . trying to fool La Legion Etrangere . . . five minutes . . . and be out with this . . . with all your dirty . . ."

Hearing this kind of raving, Castor undoubtedly recognized his superior. Sarcastically, he inquired, "Dutchy, what are the wishes of this gentleman with the inflated ego? Does he want to teach us some unprintable words?"

"We'll have to be out the gate within five minutes," I said, "because he claims we bypassed him, or one of his superiors— who knows?"

By now, the mechanics had also disappeared. Meanwhile, the colonel had thought up a whole new batch of obscenities.

"Let's get back to more civilized surroundings," Castor ordered. "All this man does is draw breath and salary. Come on, let's all push. My head is already as big as these barracks."

Quickly we gathered all the loose parts of the engine and pushed the truck out of the workshop, past the barracks, and through the gate. Our departure was a few degrees less triumphant than our entry that morning.

We put the truck back together as best we could, and it worked, though no better than before.

After five more days of engine trouble and long delays, we turned onto the road to Ain Sefra, the "Gate to the Desert." Dan and I sat in the truck's cabin, straining our eyes to see more clearly in the dim headlights that probed the inky blackness.

"Look over there, Dan," I pointed off to our right, "See those lights? Couldn't be Ain Sefra yet, could it?"

Dan peered at the faint, twinkling lights on the distant horizon. He shook his head. "Couldn't be, Dutchy. But where, for Pete's sake, are we?"

I shrugged. "We'll know when we get there. We must be on the wrong road. The map shows no village of any importance for a hundred miles or so."

For a while we kept quiet. The *Desert Rat* rattled on over

the horrible road. I drove, trying to avoid ruts and holes; but when I missed one hole, the truck slid into another.

The distant lights got nearer, as the rest of the party slept on the luggage behind us.

I drove through the main street of the village. Small alleys branched off to right and left, filled with colorless houses which appeared to have crept together for warmth on a cold night. They were the Arab Quarter, the Souk.

"There's a name on that shop," Dan said, pointing. "Geryville. Geryville? Never heard of it. Have you?"

"No. Let's stop and look at the map. Maybe this is one that's waiting to be discovered."

I stopped the *Desert Rat* in the center of the street. Dan opened the door and jumped out with map in hand. I followed, turning up my collar against the icy wind. We couldn't find Geryville on the map, which we studied by the headlights of the truck.

Finally Dan found it. "Look, here it is," he said.

"How on earth did we end up here?" I wondered. "We must have left the main road hours ago."

"It must have happened during that storm," Dan said. A short but heavy thunderstorm had struck us during the night. Rain had come down in torrents. The windows blurred and we couldn't see more than a few yards ahead. But Dan had pushed on so that we wouldn't lose still more time.

It was senseless to make reproaches. We would have to see how to get back to the road to Ain Sefra. Dan had the same idea, for he said, "There must be a back road from here to Ain Sefra. The map shows a road here. If we take it, at least we won't have to go all the way back."

"Just say we've taken kind of a detour, right?" I winked.

"We'd better get started right away," he said. "I'm freezing to death. Whoever said Africa is a hot country never spent a night in Geryville." Shivering, we climbed into the front seat again.

At about four o'clock in the morning, dark forms of mountains were vaguely noticeable against the sky to the east. *The last chain of the Atlas Mountains*, I thought. The moon had already set and only a few stars were visible. The stars were strikingly large; their bright glow was the only warmth in this naked darkness. A sudden gust of wind from behind the mountains made the sand and dust whirl around us.

Soon we found the narrow road we thought would take us to Ain Sefra. It was in terrible condition, and the terrain was getting rougher. Boulders showed up everywhere. There were more holes than road surface. Some of the holes were so deep the amber beams of our headlights disappeared when we dropped in them. Driving faster than ten miles an hour became impossible.

For another hour the truck edged forward. James took over the driving, I sat by the door on the passenger's side, and Dan sat in the middle. I tried to sleep but couldn't. Every time the truck lurched, I fell on top of Dan or against the door.

A little knock overcame the constant rev of the engine. I couldn't place the knock and still wasn't sure that it came from the engine rather than from the rocks in the road.

Suddenly there was a snapping noise and the truck shuddered and came to an abrupt halt. Everyone was instantly wide awake. One after the other we jumped out and began to investigate. Dawn was breaking on the horizon. A cold wind as sharp as a razor cut through our clothes. I snugged my arms against my body and shoved my hands deeper into my pockets but still shivered with cold.

We gathered around the open hood, but no one could find the problem. The engine kept her secret.

"That son of a . . ." Castor cut himself short of an oath. "It *would* have to go here in the middle of nowhere. We must push this heap of junk. Women and all. Get behind the truck and shove it till you tear the rocks out of the ground."

Swiftly he leaped inside and positioned himself in the driver's seat. The remaining six of us pushed as hard as we could, and as soon as the *Desert Rat* picked up some speed, Castor tried to start her in second gear, but again all we heard was a banging noise.

We pushed on to where the track began a downward slant and the *Desert Rat* picked up more speed. When Castor let out the clutch and gave the engine gas, there was a sharp, thunderous report from the engine, which died slowly away to nothing. Immediately in front of us was a sharp rise, and however hard we pushed, the truck wouldn't move another inch. It had stopped for good. Castor then swore like a madman. When he had exhausted himself, we all climbed back in the truck, numbed with cold.

For five minutes no one said a word; the only sound was the roaring wind whistling through the truck's canvas top. Castor grabbed his bottle of brandy, which always rested within his reach, and emptied the contents in one long swallow.

When he finished, he wiped his mouth with his sleeve, opened the door, and hurled the bottle at a rock.

"Where are we?" he asked Dan, who was looking at the map. "Let me have a look." Dan showed him our position.

"How did we ever get on this rotten track?" Castor snarled.

"I think we got lost last night during the storm," Dan explained timidly, then continued, "and we only noticed it early this morning when we came to a small village."

"You fools!" Castor yelled at the top of his voice. "So you stupid guys can't even keep on the right road when it rains, eh? Am I supposed to stay up all night to show you where we're going?"

His swearing cut a swath through the icy pre-dawn air.

Ann moved close to her husband. Hugging him, she tried to calm him with soothing words. "Please, darling, please calm down. This is no way to start the day, my love."

With a cold light in his blue eyes, Castor pushed her away. Dan didn't venture any further explanation and the remainder of the company kept quiet.

When Castor's rage subsided a little, I said, "No one could've told where we lost the main road in the kind of weather we faced. If you had noticed that we were on the wrong road, then you could have prevented this, but you didn't. So stop blaming everyone else!"

Castor looked at me, grinding his teeth. "You bloody Dutchman! You're the one who's caused this trouble. You!

You've wrecked my truck. I'm sick and tired of you. You can go to . . . you . . ."

A new outburst of curses exploded from his lips. Then he turned and barked, "Dick, where are you? Come here, you lazy pig. Maybe we'll all starve to death before help turns up. I don't feel like turning into a skeleton yet. Now listen well, Dick. You go together with this dirty Dutchman to Ain Sefra and get some help. You hear me? Get moving, man, right away."

Dick emerged from the luggage. With sleepy eyes he looked at our leader and asked in cockney, "Do we walk all that way? How far is it?"

"You idiot!" Castor screamed. "How do I know? You'll find out for yourself. I'll give you a can of corned beef to eat. We can't spare water, but since it's cold you won't die of thirst."

When our chief saw that Dick was in no hurry, he snarled at him. "Don't loiter, you fool! See that you get to Ain Sefra and make sure that you get some kind of truck to tow us." Dick still procrastinated while his brains tried to digest Castor's orders.

James grabbed a can from our case of provisions and tossed it to me. "Don't forget your breakfast," he said with a mean look on his face. "Otherwise, you'll tell your undertaker that we made you die of hunger."

I had little time for this character, so I spat on the ground and started walking. Dick came after me.

Dolly whined, "Please hurry back with a big lorry, fellows. I hate the sight of all these rocks. Don't leave us stranded here."

Castor's voice followed us on the wind. The last words I heard from him were rather stale—"jMy head is as big as this desert." *Quite a head*, I thought, and walked on into the desert.

The wind howled over the wasteland, but fortunately it was not as cold as it had been an hour before. The sun appeared over a mountain peak, enveloping the black-grayish rock with a hazy pink and revealing a fantastic mountain chain parallel to our path. All around was nothing but stones, gravel, and rock—endless, interminable.

We were on a plateau about 4,500 feet above sea level. That was why it had been so cold. Trees and shrubs couldn't grow here, because of too little rain and too much wind. A few small sand dunes were visible and on some of them grew a few tufts of green grass, the only sign of life. Deep ravines crisscrossed the barren land, studded with enormous boulders. This must have been the way the world looked before God finished His creation.

"The earth was without form and void," the Bible says. *Exactly like this landscape*, I thought, *desolate and wild and formless.*

Dick walked silently beside me. Dragging his long legs, he adroitly avoided holes and stones. The *Desert Rat* had disappeared from view and we were alone in a harsh world. Slowly the sun rose and thawed out our stiff limbs.

The more I thought of Castor, the less I understood how I could have stuck with him these many weeks. He had starved us, abused us with his constant rantings; he had made life generally miserable for the entire party, including his wife—and now Dick and I were walking through this strange world to get help for him.

Castor considered us to be of no more value than that: to get help for him. If we never reached Ain Sefra, it would suit our leader fine. Dick had already given Castor all his traveler's checks—and without funds Dick was of no value to him. I didn't have a cent left either; and besides that, I knew too many of his dirty tricks. We continued to eat his costly provisions, and two less mouths to feed would make a big difference for Castor.

No question about it, we were expendable. To send the two of us out together might be a good way to get rid of us. No one would miss us. Who would ever look for us in this deadly country?

Still, I was glad to be walking through this stone desert instead of listening to Castor's hysterical outbursts or looking upon his mean, sneering face.

From deep within a determination welled: I would stay with this group. I would show Mr. Castor I had staying power. No, sir, he was not finished with me yet.

"How far do you think it is?" Dick's voice broke into my thoughts.

"I don't know exactly, but I'd guess about a hundred miles."

For a while Dick seemed to be calculating. Then he frowned. "That means twenty-five hours of walking."

"Sure, if we walked four miles an hour, but we won't do that with all these millions of stones on the track," I said. "But why do you say it will be twenty-five hours of walking? Don't you think we'll meet a car?"

"This track doesn't look exactly like a highway," he said. "Just look at the ground. Have you noticed any tire marks?"

Dick was right. It looked as if there hadn't been traffic on this dirt road for ages. There were signs here and there that car tires had pushed small stones into the road surface, but that could have happened weeks ago. Maybe even months.

My stomach growled. "What do you think, Dick—shall we open this can of beef? I'm getting hungry."

"Are you out of your mind?" he flared. "If we have to walk for twenty-five hours, we'd better keep it for later. Not only that, but if you start eating that stuff, you'll have a horrible thirst. Let's just keep walking and see where we end up."

Dick grew quiet again. He measured his footsteps with a steady rhythm. I decided he was right about the beef.

The sun had grown hot. White sand as fine as dust smarted our faces. My eyes hurt. They must have been red from rubbing.

"Do you think Castor will ever get us to South Africa?" Dick asked, carefully choosing his words.

I was a bit surprised at his question.

"Why, Dick? Don't you trust him?"

"I don't know," Dick said, pondering my question. "Everything seems to be against us. Castor keeps saying there's a Jonah in our party, and if you ask me, there's some truth to that.

"Since we embarked in England to cross the Channel," he went on, "we have had bad luck. There was always dissatisfaction, and things got messed up over and over again. For instance, we stayed two weeks in Paris and three weeks in Madrid, all unnecessarily. Then three more weeks in Algiers. Why? He just seemed to develop a liking for those cities."

We walked on, and Dick continued to think. "All of that,"

he finally said, "wouldn't matter much, but it's *our* time and money he's spending.

"Maybe you know already that he has 'borrowed' all my traveler's checks," he continued. "Stupid fool that I am, I couldn't refuse him. He talks too smart about mutual interest and solidarity, but in the meantime he sits comfortably in the lorry, well protected against the sun and wind, and here we are, walking to God knows where."

Having vented his feelings, Dick lapsed into silence. This was the most I had ever heard him speak.

I looked at him from the side. His angular face and big nose made sharp lines against the blue sky. His gray hair was full of sand and stood straight up like the quills of a porcupine.

We didn't walk as fast as we had early that morning. The sharp little stones which stuck under my shoe soles hurt my feet. My tongue began feeling thick and dry. Neither of us felt like talking, so, each with his own thoughts, we stumbled on.

"Dick! Look! What's that dark object? Do you see it? It's moving this way." I was almost beside myself. Dick scanned the horizon where I pointed. "Look!" I shouted. "There's a trail of dust behind it!"

Dick stopped walking. With a sigh, he sat down on top of a rock and said, "If that thing comes this way, then it will have to come past us, so it's senseless to go another step."

After watching the object several minutes, he said, "It looks like a lorry." His voice was gravelly, probably from lack of moisture.

It was indeed a truck. I began waving my arms before the driver could even see us.

A few minutes later an old truck stopped in front of us. A shabbily dressed Arab jumped down.

"What are you doing all on your own out here?" he asked in broken French.

"Have you got water?" I asked without answering his question.

"We're terribly thirsty," Dick chimed in.

The Arab disappeared into the cabin and shortly came out with two dirty water bottles. Without a word he passed them to us and in no time the water disappeared between our parched lips.

"You people stupid," he said. And he didn't grin when he said it.

"Don't you people know that only once a week a truck comes through here? Only once a week one truck, messieurs. That is this vehicle and me. This road is just about impassable for ordinary traffic, but for me it is a lot shorter to take this road to Geryville instead of the main road up north. So I come along here once a week—and here you are!"

His words sank home, but all I could think to say was, "Then we're lucky this was the day you had to make the trip."

"If I were you I would go back instantly," he said. "I'm going to Geryville where you came from. I can take you along if you want to go."

"In a way," I said, "we'd rather go to Ain Sefra. "Do you know you're hardly halfway now?" he asked. "If you keep walking the whole night and the entire tomorrow, you might have a chance of getting there. I notice you haven't got any water. And where is your food?"

The young Arab glanced incredulously at the can of corned beef which I still held clutched in my hand.

Dick didn't wait for an English translation of the conversation. "I'm going with this guy," he said, and headed for the truck.

I was right behind him.

Sitting on the torn seat next to the Arab, we jostled and bumped over the rocky road back toward the *Desert Rat*. The truck went only about as fast as we had walked.

After half an hour of complete silence and blessed rest, Dick began to express his thoughts, though haltingly.

"Here we're coming back," he said, "faster than anticipated. I'll bet Mr. Castor will receive us back with mixed feelings. On the one hand he will be pleased to see this truck, and on the other hand he'll dread having to feed us again. He's just a two-faced cheat, Dutchy. I wish I had joined the Foreign Legion in Sidi-Bel-Abbes."

"Dick, you're a better psychologist than explorer," I said.

"Now quit your character assassination and try to concentrate on what is ahead."

"All I'm doing is analyzing the situation," he said, holding tightly to the door as we passed over a rugged stretch of road. "I'm convinced that our chief evaluates human beings only in terms of economic worth. Why is it that Dan or James were not sent on this mission instead of us? Because Castor still counts on using their bank accounts. They still have some wool to be fleeced. Our wool is gone, Dutchy, so we're being discarded as useless garbage."

"Only time will tell, Dick," I said. "So far, I don't see any other way out of our predicament than to go back to Castor."

The Arab driver remained reserved. He needed all his attention on the track before him. Clenching his teeth every time the truck passed over an ugly stretch, he was in no mood for conversation. Only once in a while he announced, "You men want drink, take water. By Allah, you need drink plenty." Our ragged rescuer might not have been the best communicator, but he had his heart in the right place.

Bumping over the track, my thoughts involuntarily wandered back to the Nazi death camps and I came to the sad conclusion that, though the setting and characters had changed, the struggle for survival was still very much the same.

I recalled one incident in particular. Soon after arriving at Siegburg, an SS guard who had been overseeing our work detail approached me. "You are on the list for the next transport," he said.

I tottered on my weak legs. According to the prison grapevine, "next transport" meant extermination. Prisoners deemed unfit for work for whatever reasons were debits to be disposed of, to be shipped off to the next world. I had a hunch that the SS had me classified as a potential troublemaker. I decided to be bold. "Isn't there anything you can do," I asked, "to get me off that list?"

The SS man stared at me, pushing his cap with skull-and-crossbones emblem backward on his head. Then in the lowest voice he could muster, he said, "Make me two ladies' handbags and one wallet and I'll see that you get off the list, *du lausbube* (lousy kid)."

One SS guard with the power to preserve life or destroy it had established my ultimate value. I was worth exactly two handbags and one wallet!

Reflecting on my present situation in this awesome desert, I wondered if things were really different now. I was virtually a prisoner of a sadist in an environment just as hostile as a concentration camp. During the time the SS ruled my life, I was worth two handbags and one wallet. Under our present dictator, Mr. Castor, my value had actually decreased to half a can of corned beef.

Dick was worth the other half.

At last, far away, we saw one small light, and a little while later, two of them. They didn't move, and when we came nearer we saw they were the parking lights of the *Desert Rat*. The truck stood in the same place as when we left.

As we drove up, the entire crew was waiting outside in the cold. Even Castor himself stood with one foot on the bumper, hand under his chin, appraising the old truck in which we drove up.

They all began to talk at once.

"Good to see you made it back, fellows," Dolly shouted. "Was this ever a long day!"

Dan greeted us with a broad grin and a simple, "Welcome to nowhere, men!"

Then Ann chimed in cheerfully, "We sure missed you. Glad you're back—and with some transportation."

Even James voiced his opinion. "So you didn't splurge, eh? Brought your bully beef back with you." And then with a sneer he added as an aside, "Some pests are hard to get rid of"—leaving it an open question whether he meant us or the can of beef.

While I related our experiences of the day, Castor made two circles around the old truck, evaluating her capacity and totally ignoring the Arab in his worn clothes.

"And you think this cursed jalopy will be able to tow the *Desert Rat*? Why, for heaven's sake, didn't you get something decent? Of all the . . .wrecks in the world . . ."

51

"Man, be grateful we came back with *this* one," I said, really annoyed with him. "You would have been here another week at least if this Arab hadn't picked us up halfway to Ain Sefra. Haven't you realized that there is no traffic in these mountains?"

"Save your smelly breath, Dutchy, and hook us up," our leader barked. "There's no time to waste on words."

The Arab pulled his truck in front of our stalled vehicle, and in record time we tied a cable to her. Then the old rescue truck took the *Desert Rat* in tow.

We jolted along the narrow track back to Geryville, depressed by the feeling that this setback would bring unwelcome changes for each one of us. As the wind whistled round the rocks and swept the sand ahead of us, we kept our silence. Only Castor hissed a sharp curse every time one of the wheels disappeared into a hole.

We arrived in Geryville about midnight. I thanked the helpful Arab but he didn't seem to hear. At least he didn't acknowledge my thanks.

When he pulled his truck away, I climbed into the back of the *Desert Rat*. The best places to sleep were already taken, so I squatted by the leaky water drum and watched a lonely star in the black sky. It was intensely cold, and I couldn't sleep. I wished I couldn't think, but thoughts crowded each other in my mind. I hardly had any clothes left of the few with which I had begun this trek. Then the temperature had been pleasantly hot; now the thermometer pointed toward zero and the wind raged.

I had arrived in Africa with three pounds in my pocket. Now I didn't have a penny. If I wanted a piece of bread, I'd have to beg for it. And Castor couldn't have much money left to improve the situation. I wondered how I could get out of this hopeless mess.

The wind howled between the houses and rattled through the canvas hood above. All night I was alone with the cold, the wind, and my thoughts.

Chapter Five:

PLOTTING THE ESCAPE

Time dragged in Geryville. Days followed one another slowly. The owner of a small hotel allowed us to park the *Desert Rat* in the courtyard, and there, protected a bit against the cold wind, we dismantled the engine.

Castor wouldn't take the truck to a garage. He was still trying to save face. "We have two first-class mechanics in our party," he said. "Let them show us what they know. I'm fed up with spending money for nothing." Dick and James began loosening the nuts and bolts of the engine block.

Progress was slow, because of the cold. At night the temperature dropped to freezing, and during the day the razor-sharp wind continued to blow. To intensify our disaster, snow began to fall, making work impossible for a few days.

Dan and I performed both necessary and unnecessary errands, mainly to get away from the rest of the party. In the evening we cooked by candlelight over a kerosene stove, but our rations were cut so much that it was senseless to cook. We had to distribute the portions by the spoonful in order to avoid fighting. Now and again, we found an empty can which one of the party must have stolen from our stock to fill his hungry stomach.

We slept on the floor of a small passageway in the hotel. The owner obviously pitied us, because he allowed us to stay there without charge. The few hotel guests had to step over us to get to their rooms. There was no door to the passage, so the wind was able to follow us in and blow its frozen breath over us as we struggled for sleep.

Lying on a gray-tiled floor, we were wrapped only in our sewn-up blankets. In the corner of the passage, Castor and his wife passed the nights on the steel frame and bare springs of an old bed we had found. It went without saying that only the supreme commander had the right to sleep on springs.

After a few days in Geryville, our captain threw off all that remained of the thin layer of civility that cloaked his evil character. Now he showed who and what he really was. For days on end he was drunk, subsisting almost entirely on cognac. If someone stepped in his way, Castor hit him with a fist or threw him against the wall. He swore and cursed, sitting half the day in the only bar in Geryville and spending the rest of the time on his bed springs.

Dolly's sleeping place was on the floor next to her mother and stepfather. On several occasions we noticed that she wanted to associate more with us, but Castor limited her contact with us. Our leader made sure that mother and stepdaughter remained private property.

James, Castor's confidante, occupied the corner opposite our chief. He had made the top of a scrapped snooker table into a bed. Next to him in a single row the rest of us had taken places—Dick, Dan, and me. We were continuously numb with cold, but our boss still had no pity.

"If you really want to go to South Africa," he said, "you'll have to make certain sacrifices, you idiots." We learned not to complain about the lack of food and blankets.

At intervals, Dolly cried, "I don't want to go to South Africa. That's *your* idea. I want to get out of here and go back home to England."

She wept unashamedly. "*You* can have your discomfort and privations. *I* want to be clean and comfortable and have some dates like other girls my age." She covered her eyes and sobbed.

"Get off my back," Castor snarled. "Your stupid reason for wanting to go back home is that scatter-brained boyfriend of yours. Forget your dumb nesting instinct and enjoy Africa. When we're through with these troubles, everything will be sunshine again. *I* know what is good for you. Quit your whining."

After fatherly advice like this, Dolly usually sought her mother and poured her heart out. With Castor out of earshot,

Ann was able to console her daughter, and at times she even succeeded in encouraging her; but with her husband close by, Ann kept quiet for fear of Castor's biting tongue. She would not jeopardize her marriage at any price.

Feeling badly about her mother's inability to help her, Dolly would walk by the rest of us whispering, "I can't stand that Castor! I hate him! I hate him!"

By now we were sure that the dissolution of our convoy was nearing fast. Each day we sank deeper into utter misery. No longer did we wash ourselves or our clothing. Half the time the faucet in the courtyard didn't work. We had given up shaving. I felt sick, half-starved, and more often than not like a living ice block.

We loathed each other's faces. We were constantly on edge. No one seemed able to break the trap into which we had fallen. We lived only in the hope that James and Dick would be able to repair the *Desert Rat*.

One day when I returned from an errand, Dick quietly took me to the side of the truck and pointed with a greasy finger to the crankshaft on the floor. A large crack had split it into two pieces.

"What did Castor say?" I asked.

"He only screamed, 'My head is as big as this hotel!'" Dick said sarcastically. "And the rest of what he said you can guess."

After a lengthy flow of curses, Castor had repaired to his corner to lie down with a bottle of cognac on his chest. He was there for an hour and then disappeared, probably to the bar for more liquor.

Two days later Castor and James went north by bus in search of a crankshaft at Sidi-Bel-Abbes. The rest of us stayed behind, most of us secretly hoping that the pair would never return.

But our intrepid leader found a crankshaft and used the last of his money to buy it. Forever ingenious, he announced at his return, "From now on, there is no more money to be spent on anything. As you all know, there are no banks in Geryville, so I can't possibly withdraw any amount from my letter of credit."

He sneered at me, daring me to speak; I was still the only one who knew the value of his letter of credit.

Another long week came to an end, and misery had almost reached its culmination point. Our only hope was that the *Desert Rat* could be repaired. That could be any day now. Dick and James were tightening the last nuts on the engine, and in the afternoon Castor planned to give the truck its first trial run.

As I left the passage one morning, a man came in who appeared to be looking for someone. He was a missionary of the well-known Catholic order *les Peres Blancs* (the White Fathers), who were stationed in some of the most remote regions of Africa. They wore long white robes with leather belts, and let their beards grow.

"Could I speak to the leader of the English expedition?" the father asked in English.

"I think so," I answered. "He ought to be somewhere in this passage here."

Castor got up from his spring frame when he saw a stranger entering our hideout. Suspiciously he looked from the missionary to me.

"What can I do for you, Father?" he asked in a saccharine tone.

Slowly the father searched for the proper English words. "It has come to my knowledge," he said, "that you have had quite some difficulties with your truck. I consider it my duty to come and see people in need to determine whether I can be of help one way or another."

Castor's face lit up. He smelled money—and probably cognac. He almost succeeded in putting on an innocent face. Without uttering a single swearword, he said, "I am really glad you have come, my Father, and that you have such an interest in our expedition. Yes, indeed, we definitely have had our share of difficulties; but I reckon with some luck we will be off again tomorrow."

Dick and I looked at each other in surprise when we heard our leader talking like a civilized person.

Somewhere in the background, Dolly murmured, "What a put-on. I never knew this was an 'expedition.'"

The White Father didn't hear her. "If I can assist you in any way whatsoever," he said, "just let me know. I will do for you whatever I can."

Judging by the twinkle of surprise in Castor's eyes, he considered this man either an archangel sent especially in this hour of need—or a complete fool. He calculated the situation slowly so as not to make a mistake, then answered in an apologetic tone, "I don't think we need any spiritual help, Father, for one of our members is a Catholic, a man of the church."

Castor paused to let this fact sink into the missionary's mind, and I looked around to see who Castor was talking about.

Then Castor went on, "However, Father, you will understand that we have a little shortage of cash due to various setbacks. You know, of course, my Father, that here in Geryville there is not a single bank where I can cash a check. So you would greatly help us if you could possibly lend us a couple of thousand francs."

He had lowered the boom rather skillfully on the father. Now it was the father's turn to ponder. While doing so he scratched his long beard, then with some hesitation stated, "Let us consider this a personal matter. You see, I have a private banking account in Great Britain because I happened to be there during the war. If you can give me your word of honor that you will deposit this borrowed money into my account in England, then I'll go ahead with your request."

Our beloved leader could hardly hide his joy. "Oh, my Father! I've always known that I could count on the church. You really will rescue us from a very grave situation!"

The kindhearted missionary smiled, "It's my firm belief that it is everyone's duty to help one's neighbor in this life. It is, after all, the second commandment."

"How right you are, Father," Castor oozed with a wry smile, glancing sideways at us menacingly to assure our silence. "That's exactly how we have lived here—in perfect harmony, just helping one another. It's a real pity you've seen so little of our brotherly teamwork."

The White Father gave us all a friendly nod and looked pityingly at our dirty faces and clothes. "I'll have to go now, ladies and gentlemen," he said. "Until next time." Then addressing Castor once more, he said, "If you can come and see me at the mission tomorrow, I'll let you have the cash."

"Exactly where is your mission?" Castor inquired, his face aglow.

"At the end of the main street, behind the church," the father said. "You'll find it easily."

"Oh, yes," Castor said. "I am certain of that."

As the father made his way out, Castor called after him, "My Father, is it all right with you if I send Dan over to collect the money? Dan is our faithful Catholic, you know, and you can really trust him. I still have a lot of things to do before our departure. I know you understand."

The White Father glanced at Dan approvingly and answered, "Sure, that's all right with me. I'll wait for you tomorrow, Mr. Dan." His long robe rustled in the wind when he stepped out into the street.

Castor rubbed his hands together, elated. "Fortunately there are still some idiots in this world," he said, and he laughed almost uncontrollably, stimulated by the thought of easy money.

"You're a crook!" Dolly said. "That's what you are—a miserable crook!" Her pretty green eyes flashed with disgust.

"Shut up, you rat," Castor shouted. "I didn't ask for your opinion." And when he noticed that all of us were staring at him, he added, "Nor that of anyone else, either. Do you hear me?"

He cursed roundly, then shouted in familiar tones, "Don't gawk at me so stupidly. You'd better shove this rotten truck out of the yard and we'll see if it works."

It didn't. We pushed it through the few streets of Geryville, but the engine wouldn't crank. We pushed and pushed, and even enjoyed the pushing because it was the first time in days that we had been warm. Castor held the steering wheel, abusing everyone verbally. He urged us to push harder. "Faster! Faster!" he cried as if addressing overworked donkeys.

When we were so tired we could push no more, our commander went to a garage, borrowed a truck and an Arab driver, and made the driver pull the *Desert Rat* through the dirty streets.

One thing became certain: The old truck didn't have any intention of running.

Late in the afternoon Castor had the Arab push our truck once more into its old place in the hotel courtyard. A hush fell over us as he entered the passage. Darkness came early this time of year, and Dolly had lighted two candles which cast our shadows grotesquely on the walls as we moved about. Castor dropped onto his springs and absolute silence reigned except for our quiet breathing.

Seeing a thunderstorm about to break, Ann began to stroke her husband's hair. He kicked her away viciously.

"Where's my bloody brandy?" he screamed at Ann, who, like a faithful dog, handed him a nearly full bottle. Right away he began lowering its level. The stillness of death filled the passage.

Dan shivered in the corner. James rested with hands under his head on top of the pool table. Dick explored his long nose with a crooked finger, and the wind played with the little flames of the candles, nearly blowing them out.

Castor emptied the bottle and threw it in the corner. He rose to his feet and everyone followed his movements.

"You hypocrites," he hissed between clenched teeth, letting his gaze run over all of us. "I'm going to split your brains, one after the other."

"Darling, don't!" Ann cried. "Don't! Don't! Don't!" She clutched at him with both hands, hysterical.

"You stupid moron!" he exploded at her, and flung her in the same corner where he had thrown the brandy bottle. Ann crashed to the floor and remained there. She sobbed noisily, covering her eyes with both hands.

He addressed us again. "Playing a double game, are you? You miserable . . . Trying to keep me from getting to South Africa, eh? . . . You filthy pigs. I'll kick you right into the next world. You've breathed your last breath here in Geryville, and I'll start with you, you lousy double-crossing Dutchman. You'll be the first dead dog!"

He jumped toward me, stretching his enormous hands to catch me. The veins in his neck were dangerously swollen, and his bloodshot eyes predicted only evil. I ducked away from him and dove toward the doorway. I looked back and none of the others had moved an inch. An alarming thought crossed my mind: The others probably wouldn't have budged an inch if they saw him kicking the life out of me. They were petrified with fear.

Castor dove at me again, and again I evaded him and made it into the courtyard. I knew I would be the loser if he got hold of me. But he gave up. Cursing furiously, he went back into the half-dark passageway.

I walked through the quiet streets of the village. A cold wind swept my burning face. I wanted to think about getting out of this miserable hole. It was freezing again, and the sharp wind penetrated my worn clothes. Cold shivers ran up and down my back. Heavy clouds drifted through the dark sky and the Arab quarters appeared gloomy and deserted. Only an occasional bolt of light from a window fell on the street.

Suddenly I heard footsteps behind. Over my shoulder I saw two figures leaving the main street. They spoke briefly to each other, then entered the alley I was in. I pressed my body into a dark doorway. When the figures stopped near me I recognized the voices of Dick and Dan.

"Did you see which way he went?" Dick asked.

I jumped from my hiding place and faced them. "Why are you following me?" I demanded.

"We want to have a straight talk with you," Dan said.

"Come on. What do you want to talk about?" I asked. "Would you really have let me be murdered by that monster while you stood by and watched?" I was seething, shaking with rage.

"Don't be absurd," Dan said. "Under the circumstances you did the best you could; you ran and so did we. If we had inter- fered, the situation would have gotten worse. Now at least none of us are hurt. Together, we might be able to think of a way out of this mess for all of us."

"What are you driving at?"

"First, tell us why the captain has it in for you?" Dick said. "What did you do that he picks on you all the time?"

"I didn't do anything. It's because I know more than you do. I know the whole story of what he's been up to, and that's why he wants to get rid of me."

"What is the whole story?" Dick pressed for an answer.

"Well, fellows," I said, "he warned me of dire consequences if I talk. He said it would be 'the end' for me. But by now I'm convinced that he'll get me anyway, if he can. So here's exactly what he's gotten us into . . ."

With that, I shared with Dan and Dick the episode at lawyer Rasseny's office in Algiers. I also told them about the ways Castor tried to get our visas for French West Africa without being able to pay the security money.

"By now you probably realize that he doesn't have a dime left," I finished. "The last few pounds he had on his letter of credit were withdrawn in Oran. I have figured out exactly, on the basis of purchases and the amount of brandy he's had, that he is completely out of cash."

Dan and Dick looked bewildered for a moment, but remained amazingly calm.

"We guessed as much," Dan said at last, "but we had no way of proving it. The arrogant crook has taken us for a ride and we were pushovers."

No one spoke for a few moments. At last Dan broke the spell. "What are you planning to do, Dutchy?"

"What *can* I do?" I said. "I'll have to go on by myself."

"You mean to say you're not going back to Holland?"

"Not on your life, never. This is not the first time I've traveled without money."

"You have no map and no papers for most of the countries you will have to go through. How do you expect to make it?"

"I have the entire map of the Sahara engraved in my mind," I said. "I know exactly in what order the oases come."

"Can't we come with you?" Dick asked hopefully. "I don't feel like staying much longer with Castor. He'll leave us behind somewhere along the line as sure as two and two make four."

"Dick, it will be difficult enough to travel alone," I leveled with them. "I really don't know yet how I will go about it. Besides, what are we going to eat? On my own, it might be possible to scratch a living together, but to look for food for the three of us would be virtually impossible.

"The same goes for hitchhiking. By myself I can hitch a ride easily, but three of us? No, guys, forget it."

"Listen, Dutchy," Dan pitched in, "we've never been in your way, have we? You can't hold anything against us. Now, be honest. Would you leave us behind just like that? We can't help ourselves in this country. We don't know the roads and can't speak the language. The French will send us back to England the very moment Castor dumps us. Come on, Dutchy—take us along."

"I've got a brainstorm," Dick suggested with enthusiasm. "I still have a suit of clothes left. I'll sell it to the Arabs early tomorrow morning, and then we'll have some money to start off with. How about it?"

"Man, I've got an old suit, too," Dan interrupted before I could answer. "I'll put that up for sale at the Arab Market. Then look what kind of a start we'll have. Dutchy, don't be stubborn. Let's take the chance together."

"That means you're going to stick it out with me, no matter what the cost?" I said.

"We will," they answered in unison. "You can count on us."

We shook hands, knowing that this moment meant a new start for each of us.

"I feel like a new person," Dick said cheerfully.

"Let's look for a spot where we can work out further details, men," Dan suggested, his whole body shaking with cold. "We probably can sit in the back room of the bar. There's usually a fire going, and Castor won't be there tonight."

We emerged from the Arab quarter and entered the only cafe in Geryville. Dan had guessed right. No one was in the back room, and we sat there near an old-fashioned round stove. We didn't even try to talk while we thawed out, holding our hands near the stove.

"Well, men," Dick broke the silence, "I'm anxious to hear how you plan to get out of here."

"The fastest way is by bus to the north," I said. "That's the only transportation out of here."

New plans quickly shaped up in my mind.

"When we leave," I said, "we should wipe out all traces behind us. Castor doesn't need to know we're off on our own; if he gets the slightest scent he'll do everything he can to stop us. So be as inconspicuous as possible. We must try to take the road to Bouktoub. That's about a hundred miles due north of here. It's where we took the wrong turn three weeks ago. Twice a week a bus leaves here for Bouktoub—and the next one is tomorrow night."

"How can we leave unnoticed?" Dan asked. "We've got luggage, and our revered leader will surely smell a rat when we start taking our backpacks out of the truck."

"Let me explain, Dan." I had this hurdle already cleared in my mind. "Both of you sell your suits first thing in the morning. That money we'll need right away. I'll reserve the seats on the bus and pay for them as soon as you get the cash. Castor usually honors this bar with his presence every afternoon. You can be sure he'll be in for a couple of drinks tomorrow. During that time we'll go to the *Desert Rat*, dig up our belongings, and along with them about half of the provisions. There were seven of us, so a little less than half is the amount we're entitled to.

"Then we'll take our backpacks to the Arab baker in the souk and leave them there till evening. Just before the bus takes off, one of us will pick up our stuff. If Castor asks where you're going in the evening, you'll have to find some pretext to come back here; but remember, it is imperative that we vanish into thin air, for if that cursing devil finds out beforehand, he'll be capable of anything."

We listened for a while to the roaring of the wind through the chimney, and our thoughts wandered on the wings of the wind toward freedom.

What a blessed thought!

"What about that business with the White Fathers?" Dan asked. "I'm supposed to go there tomorrow and pick up Castor's money. If that loan isn't paid back, you know who'll be held responsible! I'll be the scapegoat."

"Can't you hide somewhere in the village for half an hour when he sends you out?" I asked. "Then you can tell him you're supposed to go back the next day and get the money. The next day won't come for us here; we'll be gone, and Castor will have to clean up his own dirty laundry."

"All right, then, let's leave it at that," Dan said. "Are you coming, Dick? We'd better head back for the *Desert Rat* so we won't raise any suspicion with our esteemed leader. Where will we see you tomorrow, Dutchy?"

"Wait a minute, men," I said. "There's one more item on the agenda. What about Dolly?"

I felt sorry for the girl.

"What about her?" Dick questioned, raising his eyebrows. "Interested in a little romance?"

"You mean to leave that poor girl behind in the hands of those two swindlers?" I asked, ignoring the insinuation.

"I sympathize with her more than you know, Dutchy," Dick sounded irritable. "But be sensible. At first you were reluctant to take the two of us. Now you're thinking of picking up another liability? And a female, at that?"

"Not only that," Dan said with conviction, "but if our escape doesn't work out according to plan, we'd be charged with kidnapping. Besides, I'm not sure that girl is all that ready to leave her mother's skirts.

"To put it plainly," he emphasized, "Dolly has no assets other than her pretty face; and under the circumstances good looks won't get us far. Let's use our heads, men—our venture will be difficult enough without the attractions of a beautiful woman."

Self-preservation is the overruling motive of hard-pressed men. I blamed myself for not having taken a stronger stand in favor of the girl's participation, but decided to use common sense and dropped the subject.

"See you at nine in the morning in the Arab Market," I said. "We'll make further arrangements over there."

Dan and Dick stepped outside and disappeared into the cold night. The wind virtually whipped them along the dark street.

Back at the warm stove I reviewed our new plans. That wonderful feeling of being free excited me, and in spite of the fact that I didn't own a single thing in the world, I was glad to be liberated from Castor's tyranny.

Or nearly so.

During the afternoon of the following day, I walked in high spirits up and down the main street of Geryville. So far everything was going as planned. Dick and Dan sold their suits to the Arabs; I reserved three seats on the bus. Our backpacks were the next item of business.

As usual Castor entered the bar at two o'clock. Ann went with him. None of the others were around the truck, so Dick and I climbed aboard, pulled out our backpacks and appropriated about half of the food. We then disappeared into a narrow side street and carried our belongings into the safety of the Arab bakery.

Down the street I saw Dan approaching, and to my horror James walked beside him. They were walking toward the little Catholic church. Castor wasn't taking any chances. He had sent James, his confidence man, to make sure Dan brought the money to him. There was no way he could find an excuse not to pick up the loan, not with James bird-dogging him. He would have to sign for it, too. If that happened, all the evidence would be against us. I had to outmaneuver the fox!

As fast as I could, I ran through a side street, through an alley, and approached the mission building from the back. Breathing heavily, I knocked at the door.

"Could I talk to the father who came to see the English expedition yesterday?" I asked. "It's very important!"

"Come in. I'll show you the way," the bearded man said. He went ahead of me through a white-washed corridor, knocking at the last door and stepping aside to let me enter.

The room radiated no warmth whatever. Only a narrow, well-filled bookcase covered one of the walls. Some chairs of a plain style represented the rest of the furniture. The floor consisted of large reddish tiles which felt uneven under my feet. There was no comfort, no coziness in the room.

The White Father who had made the generous offer sat in one of the chairs. He looked up and saw me and there was no surprise in his eyes. But the broad smile of yesterday had disappeared. He pointed to one of the chairs and said politely, "Please sit down, sir."

As soon as I was seated, I spilled the information. "Sir, the person to whom you promised that loan yesterday has sent two Englishmen to collect it. They'll be knocking at your door any moment, but I would advise you not to part with the cash."

"I have already decided something along the same line," he said, rather soberly. "Yesterday afternoon, I found out in the village that your organizer has borrowed money from quite a few others. Up to now he hasn't paid back a single franc. You will understand it would be foolish to risk losing the few thousand francs I can call my own."

"You're more than right," I agreed. "I came only to warn you, but I'm glad that isn't necessary anymore."

I got up to leave.

"Just a moment," he said, standing too. "Wait here a few moments. In the meantime, I'll warn my colleagues that I will be unable to see these two messengers today."

In a few minutes he returned. "Tell me," he said, "aren't you also a member of this expedition? I remember seeing you there. Why did you come to warn me?"

"To recount the whole story would be too complicated," I said. "To put it in a few words, I'm through with Castor. Two of the other members and I plan to do the crossing of Africa our own way. One of the two men who was sent over here by Castor to collect your money is Dan, the only Catholic in the party. He is one of the men who will join me this evening. If Dan received a loan from you and vanished tomorrow, it would be easy for our captain to spread the word that Dan took off with your money. The three of us want to be in the clear."

The White Father looked at me unbelievingly and then asked to hear more about our fateful trip. When I gave him a summary, he remained quiet and stared for some time through the little window at the massive forms of the nearby mountains.

"How do you plan to get through to South Africa without transportation?" he asked. "You don't own a vehicle, so you will have to walk—and that is sheer madness. Believe me,

I know the Sahara, and let me tell you that this desert is death itself. I take it that you don't have any money, either." He shook his head. "Really, if I were you, I'd go back to my own country."

"No, sir, I couldn't do that," I said emphatically. "Impossible! I've been on my way to South Africa too long now and I don't believe in giving up. Whatever happens, I *must* go on."

The White Father glanced at me searchingly, but couldn't understand that this trip had become an obsession. Even if my common sense whispered, *You'd better give up*, the urge to reach my new home had become overpowering.

"What will be your next stop?" the White Father sounded a little vague. "Have you worked out how you'll cross the Sahara?"

"Yes, we have. First, we are heading for Colomb-Bechar. After that, we really don't know yet. We hope to catch a few rides the last two thousand miles through the desert. Whether that happens remains to be seen."

"When you arrive at Colomb-Bechar," he said, "go and see Pere de la Cloche of the mission. Tell him you've come to say 'hello' from me, Pere Sauvrageot. He is an old friend of mine and you can be sure he'll help you however he can."

Suddenly a bright thought flashed through my mind. "Are there missions in all the oases of the Sahara?" I asked. "If so, do you know by any chance the names of the various missionaries stationed in them?"

Pere Sauvrageot looked down at me with a smile in his eyes, and assured me, "You guessed right. There are missions all along the route you're taking. I also know most of the Peres Blancs out there. Is it now your intention to ask me their names, so you can call on them in case of emergency?"

The persistent smile of this kind man put me at ease. He was not offended by my probing, and his attitude proved that he would not reject my sudden impulse.

"Yes, sir—exactly," I said. "It would be really helpful if we had a list of the missions through the desert and the names of the White Fathers in charge of them. We do not intend to go begging. We are prepared to live on dried dates in order to reach our goal, but a roof over our heads is essential. If you could arrange that, we would be more than grateful."

"Take a piece of paper and start writing," the missionary ordered. He didn't have to tell me twice. Within fifteen minutes I had a list of names of White Fathers from Geryville to the French Sudan.

"Bring them my regards, wherever you go," Father Sauvrageot encouraged me. "Don't be afraid to knock on their doors if you are in need of anything."

I felt uplifted as I went back down the street. This list was another step in the right direction. Our friend Castor would have fits if he found out what a start we had on him.

Chapter Six:

THE GETAWAY

At 7:30 that evening Dan and Dick entered the back room of the bar, followed closely by James and Dolly. Dan's face showed a helpless expression. It was obvious that Castor had sent the two others to keep an eye on Dan and Dick. We had anticipated Castor's absence since at this time of day he usually lay sprawled in a drunken stupor on his inner-springs.

At eight o'clock the ramshackle bus would leave for Bouktoub. We had only half an hour. Our backpacks were still in the Arab bakery and they would have to be picked up.

For a quarter of an hour we made conversation around the stove. Then I got up slowly, walked outside and looked down the road. Two-hundred-fifty yards farther down was the bus, ready to leave. I called inside, "Dan, here is the White Father who came to see us yesterday. He wants to talk to you." As Dan passed me, I whispered, "Go and get the backpacks quickly." Swaying on thin legs, he disappeared in the direction of the Arab quarters.

Somewhat reassured that all would end well, I joined the remaining three in the room behind the bar. A square clock on the wall ticked off every passing second. The hustle of the bar penetrated the room where we squatted around the hot stove. James warmed his hands, unaware of our plans. He muttered in his gravelly voice, "This heat feels good. Now a quart of whiskey and I'd feel better still."

I couldn't help answering. "You and Castor are one of a kind. Your booze and foul mouths make me sick."

Flashing her eyes, Dolly was quick on the trigger, "Never was a truer word spoken."

"Keep your big mouth shut, Dutchy," James threatened, "or I'll rewire your nerve system. What are you doing here anyway?"

We sat silently for a few minutes, and I watched the clock. I wished I could be alone with Dolly, just to tell her about our impending flight and to tell her we were sorry to leave her. I wanted to say goodbye, or something, but with James at her side, chances were slim. I would spoil all our plans.

It seemed that time had stopped. James watched Dick and me with suspicion, but we pretended not to notice.

"Why is Dan staying out so long?" Dick said. "I'll go see what's holding him up." He got up and shuffled nonchalantly past us, then through the bar toward the front door.

Five minutes crawled past. Slowly the big hand of the clock moved to five minutes to eight. James and Dolly watched the door for the return of Dick and Dan.

Holding my stomach as if something serious was about to happen, I slowly walked to the barroom door and asked casually, "Any idea where the toilets are around here?"

I didn't wait for an answer. James' cynical advice followed me: "Make sure to take care of that diaper rash, pal."

Once in the bar I made for the front door. I noticed only a few customers engaged in serious debate while sipping from their glasses. As soon as I was outside, I sprinted toward the old bus.

I reached the bus just as it started moving. One last jump! I made it! I looked past the Arabs in their striped burnooses and saw Dan and Dick sitting contentedly on the same seat. A broad grin appeared on their faces when they saw me jump on the running board.

"Are the backpacks okay, Dan?" I gasped for breath.

"Sure, Dutchy," he grinned. "Everything's safely in the back."

We rode toward freedom and unknown adventure. We had finally left Castor and the misery behind us. When the last lights of Geryville disappeared on the horizon to the rear, we promised one another solemnly to conquer or to perish together.

After the bus reached Bouktoub, we awaited the arrival of the train which would take us in a southwesterly direction to Colomb-Bechar. We bought some dried dates to appease our stomachs somewhat and passed the rest of the time in the tiny office of the station master.

In the train we found a third-class compartment where four Arabs had already taken all the room on the wooden benches, to be able to sleep and snore better. We pushed them over and sat down. The air was pungent. Dan and I put our backpacks next to us to use as pillows. One of the Arabs woke up and, apparently annoyed by our disturbance, turned off the lights. Peace then settled over the coach. The monotonous rattle of the train rocked us to sleep. Forgetting the world around us, we dreamed of better days ahead.

In the early morning, Dick's hoarse voice awoke us. I detected a touch of annoyance in it. "Hey, you sleepy heads, where's my backpack? Come on, wake up! Dan! Dutchy! Those smelly Arabs stole my luggage, sleeping bag and all!"

I looked around, still drowsy, instinctively checking whether my backpack was there. It was. Fortunately it was still stuck under my head. Dan hadn't lost anything either. Only Dick's luggage and the four Arabs had vanished. Dick was in a rage. Furiously, he walked up and down the compartment, opened one of the windows and looked outside as the train stopped in a small station. There he poured his cockney vocabulary over all the Arabs who walked past on the platform, but it didn't make his property come back.

The next day we arrived at Colomb-Bechar. This railway terminal was the southernmost point we could reach by train. From here we would have to hitch rides through the world's largest desert before we reached the Niger River in French West Africa. It seemed altogether unattainable. We had only a few francs left of the money from the suits, and the permit which would enable us to cross the Sahara would expire within a month.

We decided to pay the local White Fathers a visit. We brought them regards from Pere Sauvrageot and then carefully inquired into the possibility of receiving shelter for the night.

Everything went beyond our expectations. The fathers were extremely friendly, and when I told them something of our trip, we were offered a room in the mission where we could stay for the rest of the time in Colomb-Bechar.

We were embarrassed at so much hospitality, for it had been a long time since we had spent a night in such a comfortable place. A fireplace and electric stove in our room gave us heat. We even had the use of a small radio, but to me the most extraordinary comforts were the heavy spring mattresses, a luxury I had not known for more than a year.

One of the missionaries brought us in contact with a Frenchman, a handsome man named Marcel, whose trucking company reached several oases in this part of the Sahara. He was taller than six feet and a person of few words.

When I explained our predicament, he pointed to a large truck being loaded by some Arabs and said, "If you don't mind putting up with this kind of transportation you can sit on top of that load."

Instead of thanking him, I said, "We are not in a position to pay you anything. I hope you will not put this ride on our account."

"Money is no object," he said. "Tomorrow I am off to Adrar, about five hundred miles to the south. That means a trip of a day and a half. Be here at nine and you can come along."

We did not oversleep the next morning. Long before the truck was due to depart, we were at hand to make sure of our first long ride. Our crossing of the enormous Sahara was starting to be a reality.

On top of the high truck we watched Colomb-Bechar disappear from view. Another Arab hovel, one more scrawny date palm, a curve in the path, and a hill of rocks took away the view of the oasis. We shared our high observation post on the truck with three Arabs. Judging by their many wide burnooses, they seemed to have prepared themselves for a polar expedition. The Arab next to me wore at least three striped robes, one over another, and two extra ones lay next to him in case of still colder regions to come.

The path we followed was filled with ridges, looking more like a washboard than a road. My bowels got a real shaking, and when the truck rounded a curve we had to hold on tightly to the ropes to keep from sliding off. But no circumstances could make us unhappy—we were devouring miles and that was our purpose.

As the hours passed, the countryside changed. There were high hills, even sand dunes which rose an easy one-hundred-fifty feet above the path. Later in the afternoon, the air abruptly grew chilly. We took out our thin blankets and huddled together, trying to preserve our warmth. The three Arabs donned extra burnooses to keep warm. I had stuffed my pockets with dried dates, and while chewing contentedly, I admired a most spectacular sight: a desert sunset. The hills trailed long black shadows behind them; and the ocean of sand, which could still be reached by the sun, reflected a beautiful amber. The sky in the west showed an explosion of blazing colors from hard pink to light blue. Hastening toward the end of her daily course, the sun slowly turned into a flaming red fireball, sinking behind a quivering horizon.

We drove along a dry river bed. Low palm trees grew on the side. The farther south we traveled, the taller and slimmer the palms became.

When the last streak of sunlight was overpowered by the shadows of twilight, we reached a small oasis, Igli. Between the palm trees I saw the contours of the first little houses. It was hard to spot these low Arab hovels, and no wonder! They were the same color as the sand. One thing was certain: The inhabitants of these sand and mud structures did not have to be afraid of a sudden downpour, for the one-tenth of an inch of rain that fell during the year would be insufficient to destroy their sand homes.

A pitch black night blotted out every earthly object, but the tall Frenchman did not feel like giving up the struggle yet. Behind the wheel, he followed the long trail thrown open by the headlights, and the six of us atop the truck kept rolling and rocking on top of the load.

The Arab next to me handed us one of his wide robes for extra cover, but it didn't help much. The icy breeze penetrated everything, even the seven burnooses which one of my fellow travelers had managed to put on, and even he shivered most of the time.

It appeared that every object had turned into ice—the ropes to which we clung, the canvas on which we sat, everything. Even the glittering stars above us looked frozen, and the endless rows of sand dunes looked stark and sallow under their cold yellow light.

At midnight we reached the oasis Kerzaz, which according to the Arabs was a holy place on which *rumis* (white unbelievers) were not allowed to set foot. Some miles away from the oasis stood a lonely house where the only European of Kerzaz lived as a recluse. Marcel decided to spend the night there. He silenced the engine and called to us, "Get down, everybody. That's enough for today."

Carefully we climbed down the ropes. My knees refused to bend and my legs felt like sticks. My jaw was so stiff I could hardly talk. Dan and Dick didn't look to be in any better shape. We supported one another and stumbled to the house of the recluse. Fortunately, this loner of Kerzaz understood of the needs of a Sahara traveler. A large bowl of noodle soup stood ready for us, and eventually, when we had swallowed as much of it as we could, our body temperature returned to normal. In the corner of the room were two mattresses where the three of us passed the night.

Next morning, not many words were spoken as we took our seats next to the three Arabs on top of the truck. We all thanked the loner of Kerzaz, a European who had given up the fast life for the solitude of the desert.

We followed the dry river bed, and the desert became the way I had always pictured it to be—a yellow ocean full of huge sand waves, drenched in the harsh light of a pitiless sun.

The deeper we penetrated the Sahara, the more we descended, for the region directly south of Algeria dipped about one hundred feet below sea level. Farther to the east, in the most central part of the desert, were the Hoggar Mountains, a rocky plateau with peaks reaching 6,000 feet into the copper sky.

During the afternoon, the landscape turned flatter. Once in a while we could see a small dark patch on the horizon. It would always turn out to be a forest of date palms, and along the edges in their shade, a sleepy settlement. Slowly we left the area of the moving dunes, and the track we followed became straighter because it didn't have to curve around the dunes anymore.

Marcel drove rather fast, there being no reason with the straighter road to keep the speed down. Dan, Dick, and I didn't talk much to one another. We were too awed by the grandiose scale of the emptiness around us—a total repression of all life in a measure only God Himself could have contrived.

I was relieved when we finally arrived at the oasis of Adrar. From here we would have to look for another ride through the remaining part of the Sahara. We faced the last barricade, a barrier of fifteen hundred miles of sand and endless stretches of bare hardpan separating us from still darker Africa.

Chapter Seven

THE TANEZROUFT, LAND OF THIRST

"After pestering almost every living creature in Adrar about bumming a ride through the Sahara," Monsieur Lidon said scaldingly, "—which by the way is forbidden by law—you've come to see me, have you? . . ."

He waited a moment to be sure his point was taken, then continued in the same self-assured tone: ". . . while *I* as representative of the Trans Sahara Company am actually the only person who could have assisted you in your efforts to cross the Tanezrouft."

Again he waited, seated smugly behind his desk, and looked in turn at Dan, Dick, and me. When he was convinced that we fully realized his importance, he took to lecturing again.

"*I* represent the only company which has authority to transport people through this part of the desert, and if you would . . ."

"Just a moment, Monsieur," I interrupted. "It wouldn't have made any difference if we had come to see you first. We don't have a dime between the three of us and that's why we try to travel the cheapest way possible—which means hitchhiking, of course. There was no other way for us. I know it sounds silly to come to you after we inquired everywhere else first, but in our position one sometimes does things one wouldn't do under normal circumstances."

The Frenchman managed a weak smile, then picking a file out of one of his desk drawers, he said slowly, nodding his head, "Perhaps you care to know how the Trans Sahara Company back in Colomb-Bechar feels about you? Here is a special file with items pertaining to you. Look here, I have filed it under the caption *Les Anglais et le Hollandais* (the Englishmen and the Dutchman). Just go ahead and have a look at these papers. You will get an idea what I can still do for you."

He placed the file in front of me. A little startled by his statement, I studied the sheets of paper. They consisted almost entirely of telegrams. Lacking a telephone system in this part of the world, the Trans Sahara Company used the company telegraph. The first part of each wire usually pertained to company business, but at the end of each telegram a few short lines followed concerning the three of us.

Two of the footnotes read:

Take your precautions! Don't let them go any farther.

Have them sent back at the first available opportunity.

The last words of each telegram were always the same, like the monotonous beat of a native drum: "Watch out for the Dutchman! Watch out for the Dutchman! Watch out for the Dutchman!"

Monsieur Lidon watched me until I had devoured the words on every telegram. He then asked cynically, "Any comment perhaps, Monsieur?"

Astounded, I was unable to utter a word. It was more than obvious that we had a bad name in this office, in spite of the fact that we had been in Adrar only a short week and had been in Colomb-Bechar less than that. We had not done anything out of the ordinary; we had lived on dried dates, water, and bread the whole time here, and we had been in no trouble.

"Could you explain the meaning of all this?" I demanded.

Lidon seemed glad to be able to talk again. "In case you don't know it yet," he said, twisting one corner of his mouth as he spoke, "your name stinks here."

He underlined that statement. He was agitated, and to occupy his hands he began cleaning his nails without looking at them.

"It must be disappointing to find out we know so much about you here in Adrar, isn't it?" he said. "These Englishmen," he pointed to Dan and Dick, "could be decent citizens. I'm convinced we would let them go if they had the money to pay their fares; and, of course, if they would not associate with you. But we're after you, Monsieur le Hollandais—or do you feel like denying that you spent years in camps during the war because you're a communist? And have you forgotten already that you're earmarked as a deserter? What about that money you stole from your friends a few weeks ago back in Geryville?"

Bingo! The light dawned. Castor!

"As you see," the Frenchman continued, "we might be living here in a remote corner of the globe, far from civilization; but even here the truth eventually overtakes lies."

He paused to let the accusations sink in. For a moment I stood crushed, but instinctively I knew the accusations had come from Castor. He would not want me to reach British territory, if only out of fear that I might be a witness against him in a court case. I should have suspected that he would try to make travel difficult for us. I found it hard to contain myself. I looked Lidon straight in the eyes and managed to say calmly, "Seeing that you seem to believe all these accusations, sir, you will have to give me a chance to defend myself. That's the only right I've got left."

Without giving the man before me a chance to interrupt, I started telling about my past. I told him about the years I spent in camps and prisons during the war, emphasizing the fact I was sentenced to ten years hard labor, not because I was a communist, but because I tried to join the Dutch in England to free my country. I continued about the trip through Africa, my meeting with Castor, and about his dirty tricks, and that at the end we *had* to leave him because it was impossible to travel any farther with a madman.

Dan and Dick confirmed the latter part of my story.

"I don't expect you to believe this," I continued, "but you will be convinced by the proof I carry on me. This is my membership card in a society for veterans in Holland, and here is my passport. In it is a valid visa to cross the Sahara. That's exactly the same visa as my English companions received in Algiers. You can't believe that these documents were forged, can you?"

Lidon had finished cleaning his nails when I ended my speech. He blew his nose and remarked, "What you've just told me gives a different perspective to the case, of course, if your little story is true. Nevertheless, even if you had the money to travel in the most luxurious way, I couldn't help you. What I could do is send a telegram to headquarters in Colomb-Bechar to clarify the whole situation. Perhaps the Lordships over there might change their hostile policy if they know you are in possession of visas and other valid documents. Come back in a day or two and then I might be able to give you a more definite answer."

A little later we strolled across the dusty, huge square that took up a hundred thousand square yards of desert space.

"My head is as big as this square," Dick imitated our former leader, spitting a date pit into the sand. We all laughed, venting our emotions. Dan's shoulders sagged more than usual and he looked extremely tired.

We walked up and down the enormous square the rest of the afternoon, which was what we had been doing every afternoon for a week.

Our reception at the White Fathers mission in Adrar had been a rather cool one, though we were permitted in the foyer where we could sleep on stone benches for the time being.

The day after we arrived, we had gone to work immediately, contacting all persons (and they were few) and all companies (they were fewer still) who owned cars, inquiring whether they planned a trip farther south in the near future. No one gave us a hopeful word.

When the few car owners got wind that we were after a free ride, they cut their conversation with us instantly, telling us, "If you have a free ride in mind, you'd better go and see the Trans Sahara Company. Not that it has a charitable mind, but it has a monopoly on all transport. The company would make us pay a handsome fine if it found out we had taken anyone along; and it wouldn't make any difference whether we made you pay for the trip or not."

The mighty arm of the Trans Sahara Company was all-powerful. Everyone feared it.

The only person who showed us real sympathy was the captain of the Foreign Legion. As the commander of Adrar, it was his duty to check every individual entering or leaving the area. We had to report to him the morning after our arrival, and as could be expected, our presence in Adrar was not really wanted. The permit for the Sahara that we had in our passports was a mere transit visa, and valid only if we used our own transportation or that of the Trans Sahara Company.

The captain gave me the opportunity to explain how we had arrived at Adrar. When I finished telling my story, he got up and paced the big room. Suddenly he stopped in front of me and said in a firm tone, "Of course I have to send you back, young man . . . but if you disappeared . . ." He shrugged his shoulders and said no more.

"Merci, mon capitaine," I hurried to say, understanding exactly what he was suggesting. There was a smile in his eyes, but, unbending in his manner, he said not another word.

The days came and went for us without bringing any change in our situation. But considering that we were stranded halfway between Algiers and Gao on the south side of the Sahara, time didn't really make that much difference. Perhaps tomorrow . . .

On our eleventh day in Adrar, we once again saw Lidon of the Trans Sahara Company. This time he was polite and businesslike, without arrogance. "I received a wire from headquarters a little while ago," he said with more sympathy in his voice than I had anticipated. "In short, this is what has been decided about you. You will be allowed to travel with our company through the remaining part of the Sahara on condition you pay your fare—and the fare for the three of you will be forty-four thousand francs. Besides this, we require a warranty of one hundred thousand francs. Simple addition will tell you that this crossing will cost you one hundred and forty-four thousand francs."

All we had left in francs was the price of a good meal in an ordinary restaurant. As Lidon studied our clearly hopeless faces, his businesslike attitude disappeared and the warm temperament of a real Frenchman surfaced.

"I'm very sorry, gentlemen," he sighed, "but believe me, I can't do anything about it."

He dutifully filed away the decisive wire that made further travel through the Sahara appear impossible for us.

Without a word we left his office, but all hope was not yet gone. There was still the captain of the Foreign Legion. I tried to convince myself that there was some chance they would send us on to Nigeria. Nigeria was about as far away as Algiers. If the Foreign Legion received orders to remove us from the area, they might as well get rid of us in the direction we wanted to go! Our deportation expenses would work out about the same, whether on to Nigeria or back to Algiers.

But a second blow, deadlier than the first, awaited us in the captain's office. The rigid soldier did not beat around the bush. "I have news for you," he said. "Today I have received orders from higher up." I could tell he was choosing his words carefully. "My orders are as follows: I have to send you back with the person who brought you here. Next Monday one of his trucks will be going north. You will have to leave Adrar aboard that truck. I hope it will not be necessary to stress the importance of your being on time."

We left his office quietly. We all understood that the inevitable moment had come.

To sort out our thoughts, we went for a stroll along a narrow path through the enormous palm grove of Adrar. I had expected a terrible outburst of anger from my friends, but strangely enough, they remained composed. I too was rather composed. The tension was gone. We had to go back. The order was irrevocable. Each of us had submitted to the verdict with a resignation that was natural to the Arabs. Perhaps we finally realized the absurdity of all our plans.

When we had walked past the last palm trees, there were only the short waves of the open sand sea ahead, the majestic but relentless desert. A little to the right was an old fortress, possibly from the days when the Romans were lords of the Sahara. Dilapidated and partly covered by sand, it lay there forever baking in the sun. We had explored it on other walks, but not today. Our attention was riveted on the sand, the ocean of white-yellowish sand that neither one man nor three could ever cross unaided.

Walk through fifteen hundred miles of sand, sinking ankle-deep with every step? And if the Arabs saw you, they would tell. When told, the Foreign Legion would be sent to look for you, and they would have no trouble finding. They would bring you back dead or alive.

We had condemned ourselves to failure the moment we decided on the Sahara route.

Veni . . . Vidi; I came . . . I saw . . . and I was defeated.

Two days later I paced up and down the sandy square of Adrar, my mind a blank, incapable of thought. I had left Dan and Dick sleeping on the stone benches of the mission. Each in his own way was simply existing through the hours until Marcel took us north again.

"You have problems?" a voice brought me up short. I turned to look into the face of an Arab in a white burnoose. His complexion was a few shades darker than that of most Arabs in North Africa. A clean turban had been superbly wrapped around his head.

His question annoyed me a little. I was in no mood for Arab curiosity, so I answered briefly, "Yes, quite a few."

Pacing close beside me, he continued in the dignified manner so natural to the Arabs, "If by chance your difficulties are of a financial nature, I probably would be able to help you."

I stopped and looked more closely at him. I felt my eyes blink; I felt as if I had been hit over the head. "Wh-what is th-that?" I stuttered. "Do you mean that?"

"I would not make this statement unless I meant it," he said quietly. "If you can prove that you have money in Nigeria and that you are willing to pay it back over there to a friend of mine, I will advance you the cash which the Trans Sahara Company requires of you to cross the Tanezrouft."

I could not believe my ears. I stood totally dumbfounded. Then I got my brain in gear. Once in possession of this money, we could remove all obstructions. Dan was the only one of us who had a bank account in Nigeria. I was already quite sure he would advance Dick and me the money we would need to repay this Arab.

I looked more closely at this man who was coming to our rescue and recognized him to be one of the two men who were always sitting behind the counter of the shop where we bought dried dates every day. How did he know our need? I was still at a loss as to how I could thank this Arab nobleman.

"By helping us you would really get us through the darkest hour of this trip," I began, "and you must believe that I've hardly ever been so grateful to anyone in all my life. I first want to convey your offer to my friends, because one of them has a bank account in Kano, Nigeria. I am convinced that he will go along with your proposal."

He nodded as if he was quite indifferent to whether these strangers accepted his money or not. "*Entendu* (that's agreed)," he said. "If your friend agrees, then you can find me in the shop of Ben Yusef. By the way, my name is Mustafa."

As fast as my feet would carry me, I ran across the square to the mission building.

"Dan and Dick," I said, "you won't believe me, but listen to what happened . . ." I plunged at once into the matter. The Englishmen looked at me a little annoyed; but when I told them about the offer of the mysterious Arab, they became excited as well.

Dan was first to put his thoughts into words. "Well, what are we hanging around here for?" he asked. "Let's go see this Mohammedan Prince Charming. I'll dig up proof that I really have an account in Nigeria, and don't worry, I'll pay for you guys too—if you feel inclined to pay me back some day."

Dick and I assured Dan that we would reimburse him as soon as we could.

Fifteen minutes later we stood at the counter of Ben Yusef's little grocery shop. The owner smiled knowingly when he saw us enter. With a slight nod of his head he winked toward

Mustafa, who sipped unperturbed from a small glass of black coffee. Slowly Mustafa rose and made his way to the counter. I told him that Dan was quite prepared to contract for a loan. Then I handed him the evidence of Dan's investment in Kano.

Mustafa glanced casually at the document and remarked, "This is fine, Messieurs. Just make out an IOU to me, and a promise of payment to Mr. Wafoedin in Kano."

Dan took pen and paper and made up a contract. In the meantime, Mustafa spoke softly in Arabic to Ben Yusef, who handed him a pile of banknotes from a drawer beneath the counter.

When Dan completed and signed the document, he showed it to Mustafa. Without expression, the Arab folded it and tucked it away in the folds of his burnoose.

"I will forward this paper to Wafoedin in Kano," he said. "He will know then to expect you."

He pushed the pile of banknotes to Dan. "I hope this will give you another chance," he said. And he sounded as if he meant it.

As we were leaving, he walked to the door with us. "When you have reached Gao, come and see me if you are in need of anything. Gao is my hometown. Just ask around for Mustafa Saada. Anybody there can tell you where I live."

"Your hometown?" I asked. Gao is on the other side of the Sahara.

"That is correct," he said. "Within a few days, I, too, will cross the rest of the Tanezrouft with the Trans Sahara Company—back to my home." Crossing the largest desert in the world was apparently routine for him.

I felt a bit apprehensive about this generous aid. No European had helped us to such extent on any part of our trip, and certainly no one else had offered so much help during this dark hour when we needed help the most. Very few Europeans could or would have understood our position; but this Mustafa, son of a different culture, had offered help without even asking what kind of help we needed.

Incredible! The more so since in the eyes of a Mohammedan we could only be contemptible unbelievers. Whatever prompted his actions, Mustafa was a God-sent Good Samaritan in Arab garb.

Five minutes after we put the money in our pockets, we stood on the threshold of Lidon's office. He was obviously suspicious as he counted our cash. He squirmed, clearly perturbed by the thought of having to make an independent decision about us.

Finally he said, "I will have to wire headquarters and we will see what *they* have to say."

So we left his office without attaining our passage. It seemed inconsistent to us that we couldn't even get rid of the money which our Arab friend had so readily lent us. One thing was certain: Our hope and courage had returned. It was unthinkable that the Trans Sahara Company would refuse us passage.

When I told the White Fathers the story of our good fortune, the older of the two smiled and said with some irony, "Yes; this Mustafa can afford a little gift like that. He is rolling in money."

"What kind of a person is he?" I asked.

"He is one of those influential merchants who have trade relations over most of North and West Africa," he explained. "The man owns camel caravans that cross the desert. He has large herds of cattle grazing on the grassy plains near the Niger River. He trades in narcotics, slaves, and ivory, and he would not go home from a trip like the one he is now on unless he had made a couple of million francs."

"He sounds like one of those romantic pirates out of the Middle Ages," I said.

We were quiet for some time, and then I ventured to ask, "All the things you mentioned a little while ago—the narcotics, slaves, ivory, and the like—aren't they against the laws of this country? How does he go about those dealings?"

"Of course all such things are prohibited," the White Father responded, "but trade deals like these are negotiated only between a very few people who are trustworthy to each other. As far as slaves are concerned, they are mainly Negroes from West Africa. The slave traders operate mostly in Muslim countries, so it isn't that easy to trace their various offenses. Then again, these slaves are considered more as servants than personal property. They don't lead the same kind of life as their relatives of earlier times who were shipped to the Americas like matchwood."

Our host obviously had strong feelings on this subject and did not touch on it again.

That night, the stone benches on which we slept seemed to be less hard and much more comfortable than before.

As we relaxed the next afternoon, a barefoot Arab boy in tattered clothing knocked softly on the door of the mission. "Monsieur Lidon sends this," he said, handing me a note. He then disappeared as silently as he had come.

The note was addressed to "The Englishmen and the Dutchman," and inside was a terse message: "I have something important. Come and see me."

In a matter of minutes we arrived at Lidon's office, fully expecting him to say that all red tape was slashed and we were free to continue southward.

But after the customary "Bonjour, Messieurs," he picked up a telegram from his desk and handed it to me. "Do you know any of these people?"

A glance at the telegram told me trouble lay ahead. "Tomorrow with Bus Eighteen," the telegram read, "will arrive: Mr. B. Castor, Mrs. A. Castor, Miss D. Samson, and Mr. James Potter."

I told Dick and Dan what the telegram contained, and Dan shouted, "I told you I knew where our present troubles stem from!"

We began to ponder all angles of our situation, past and present.

"It's clear," said Dan, "that Castor is the one who's been spreading lies about us. But why did the last response of the Trans Sahara Company only mention amounts of money needed for the crossing? Nothing more has been said about sponsorship, crimes, or anything else. Now this surprise."

Dick brought up another interesting question. "Tell me,

Dutchy, why is it that Castor and the others are apparently being allowed to cross the Sahara and we're being held? They have exactly the same transit permit we have, and their money is no better than ours. The Trans Sahara Company keeps bothering us about security money. What about them? The same person who sponsored Castor sponsored us. If they can travel on, why can't we?"

Lidon stood quietly near the window while we talked in English, a language he couldn't understand; though now and then he must have guessed what we were talking about.

Sinking in the only armchair in the tiny office and clutching the ominous telegram, Lidon stated ominously, "If it has per chance entered into your minds that you're going to take revenge on a person traveling by Trans Sahara Company, then your last hope to ever cross this desert is gone. You'll have to understand that if you're going to cause me any more trouble, I will not lift another finger for you. Don't act so simple now as if you didn't intend to do anything at all about this Castor once he has arrived here, for I can see the thirst for blood in your eyes."

"Monsieur Lidon," I said, "you know very little about the things this man has done to us. Castor has violated every principle of decency and morality. Why does your company favor this kind of person over us? Let's be honest. The authorities here are playing with us as if we are the balls on a pool table. Do you think for a moment we appreciate that? Do we have fewer rights than this individual, and is his money cleaner than ours?"

Arguing back and forth, the Frenchman concluded that we weren't making much progress. After a deep sigh he made an unexpected move.

"Messieurs," he said with resolution in his voice, "we have to come to an agreement. If you simmer down, I have a proposition to make. I feel somehow that you haven't gotten a fair deal. That's why I'll promise you faithfully to give you all possible assistance at my disposal to enable you to cross this desert on one condition only: Hands off Castor while he's here in Adrar."

Though Lidon saw we weren't very impressed with his way of reasoning, he continued, this time frowning: "It would be sheer madness to tackle Castor, just plain suicide. You have, as far as I can see, valid visas; and as of yesterday also the necessary cash to travel. You would destroy all your chances if you touched this man. Messieurs, use your brains. The only thing you still need is the evidence that this person in Algiers was your sponsor also. After that, you'll be hopping through the desert like three kangaroos."

"The evidence you're looking for is in our passports," I replied coldly. "The Algerian government does not issue transit visas for the Sahara if one isn't backed by recognized security. The person who served as our guarantor is called Rodriguez, lives in Algiers, and owns a garage. As far as I know, Castor doesn't have any written evidence of this. He went with Rodriguez alone to the Visa Department and came back with visas for the seven of us."

After briefly meditating, Lidon said, "I am considering my own approach to this Castor fellow. I just need a chance to review his papers."

"If you don't mind spending a few francs on liquor," I said, "the man and his secrets are yours." I explained that Castor was a total drunk.

"You must understand that I have no official right to interrogate passengers of the company about the kind of documents they carry," Lidon resumed. "On the other hand, you men deserve some, shall we say, irregular cooperation; but only on the condition that you stay completely out of it—out of sight. I must have this assurance."

Clearly there was no alternative for us. "You have our assurance," I said. We were confident of a favorable outcome from Lidon's review of Castor's papers. He would see, when going over the passports, that our visas were all the same, with consecutive numbers.

Once more we marched across the square with its two-thousand-year-old wells and on to the home of the White Fathers. Wherever we went, Castor's name clung to our thoughts.

It was almost nine o'clock, and the huge square of Adrar slumbered dark and deserted in the vast Sahara night. Clusters of stars glittered in the cold, black sky. A few notes of an Arab flute floated in the air. The only lights to be seen were in the lounge of the miniscule hotel of Adrar.

Dan I moved furtively toward the half-open window that looked into the front of the lounge. Carefully lifting my head just high enough, I looked inside. There he sat—Castor, the swindler! His narrow, bloodshot eyes wandered restlessly from one person to the other. In his hand he clamped a large glass filled with cognac, and at regular intervals he took a long sip.

The others—Ann, Dolly, James, and Lidon—sat opposite him. On the table between them were various half-filled glasses of liquor waiting to be disposed of. Ann and Dolly were silent. James emitted an occasional growl as if in pain; we couldn't make out his words. It was clear that Castor and Lidon were monopolizing the conversation, which because of the language barrier consisted mostly of sign language.

In silence, as we watched the spectacle, involuntary disgust got the better of us. If only that Frenchman could get hold of the papers in Castor's leather case. If only he could have one glance at Rodriguez's affidavit.

In the lounge, the game of trying to understand one another went on. The glasses were filled again and again.

I stared at Ann and Dolly. "Really," I whispered to Dan, "those two women are the only ones worth talking to."

"Yes, they're all right," Dan agreed softly. "I wish we could do something for them; but the problem is they're tied down to the wrong fellows."

For the next ten minutes not a single noise stirred the stillness of the night.

"Won't Lidon ever get in the act?" Dan broke the silence with an impatient whisper.

Then with sudden shock I realized that Castor might very easily out-drink the Frenchman, for it would take our former leader more than a dozen drinks to reach the saturation point.

An Arab boy walked past, and at the same time I got a bright idea, "Just a moment," I whispered to the boy "Would you mind taking a note to the gentleman of the Trans Sahara Company? He's right inside there."

I had already dug up a piece of paper and jotted down in a hurry: *Come outside as soon as you can. The Dutchman.* Together with the note I pressed a couple of francs into the hand of the Arab boy. He slipped through the front entrance of the hotel. I wanted to advise Lidon to hurry and get Castor's visa numbers checked out, because at the rate the Frenchman was going, he would drink himself into a stupor and nothing would be accomplished.

Dan and I withdrew to the porch of an adjoining house in case Castor and his followers took a notion for some fresh air too.

We watched but no one appeared in the doorway of the hotel. No Lidon, and no Castor. A cold wind swept along the porch where we hid. I shivered in my thin clothes. A plaintive tune of Arab music quavered on the cold air stream.

Waiting and hoping was more than aggravating. Over there, only a few yards away, sat the man who had caused us so much misery. After apparently having sold the *Desert Rat* for cash in Geryville, he now had money to spare. *He* could afford a soft bed to sleep in. *He* could sit in any restaurant and enjoy a juicy steak. He could even afford to warm himself on brandy. The fact that bothered us most was that he could travel in a luxurious bus. If we could only empty Castor's pockets to prove to Lidon that he traveled on exactly the same permit as we did! But we had promised the Frenchman on our word of honor not to interfere and to leave everything to him.

And now, if Castor had a notion to be obstinate and Lidon didn't get to see any of his documents, the authorities would send us back to Europe.

After we lingered for another hour near the entrance of the tiny hotel, it became obvious that Lidon had decided to totally ignore my message.

"What? Do you mean to say that you let that villain go?" I shouted unbelievingly when we finally met with Lidon in his tiny office the next morning.

"Yes, old Castor left for good," he said. "He and his friends are on the Sahara bus on their way south. So is your friend Mustafa Saada; he left on the same bus."

"Were you able to get hold of Castor's leather case with the documents?" I asked, growing more impatient by the minute.

"Oui, Messieurs, I did," he said. "It cost me quite a few rounds of drinks before I was able to convince Castor to let me have a look at his papers. Now concerning this question of permits: Their permits are exactly the same as yours. They were all issued on the same date and their numbers and yours run in sequence. You were right about that, but I found no evidence of your having the same sponsor. You probably haven't been able to travel because you have been too much of a nuisance."

Lidon was not in his usual cheerful mood. He stared absentmindedly out the window over the empty square. A minute went by in which no one spoke. When we finally made for the door, Lidon stopped us and said rapidly, as if he didn't want to be interrupted, "That was not all. There is something else I wanted to tell you. This morning I received a wire from headquarters which contains good news for two of you, and rather bad news, I am afraid, for the other. I'm sorry, my friends. Now it is impossible for me to help you any further. This telegram decides the entire issue once and for all."

Pronouncing the last words solemnly, he pushed one of the well-known telegram forms into my hands. I snatched the piece of paper from him, knowing that I was "the other" of the three, and devoured the following words: "Two Englishmen Can Leave. Dutchman Can Only Travel On Condition Paying Additional 34,000 Francs Security."

I couldn't say a word. Whole paragraphs were stuck in my throat.

Dan and Dick were alarmed. They insisted, "What is it? What is written there? Come on, Dutchy, we want to know too. What's the matter?"

In a toneless voice I repeated, "Two Englishmen can leave. Dutchman can only travel on condition . . ." I ran outside to the oversized square and could only think of Castor's words: "My head is as big as this square."

Dan and Dick followed me. Again we walked, silently now, through the dust and sand of the oasis.

"If you have to go back, I go back too, Dutchy," Dan's voice came as if through a heavy fog.

"Are you crazy?" Dick remarked, more animated than he was by nature. "That would be throwing away your chance, and the best one we've had so far."

"I won't let Dutchy down," Dan said emphatically. "You remember while leaving Geryville only a month ago, we promised to be faithful to one another. Well, let's stick to that promise. If *he* has to go back, we *all* go back."

"And lose this opportunity?" Dick said without too much conviction. "I think we've done what we could."

Their arguing brought me back to reality. Dick was right. What use was it if they waited for me, just to see how I would be sent back? Whatever could I scrape together? Certainly not thirty-four thousand francs.

My spirit and courage were defeated. All my trying was in vain, though I had done the utmost to reach my goal. Many times my throat had been hoarse from talking. My sandals were worn out from walking back and forth to various companies and countless persons. I had put up with a hard bed, a meager ration of dates and bread, and many a hardship to reach South Africa. What was the outcome? Just nothing, plain nothing.

At the insistence of the White Fathers and Lidon, Dan, at last, decided to take the opportunity to cross the rest of the Sahara. The inconsistent Trans Sahara Company might change its mind. To show his good will, Dan left me one third of Mustafa's money, just in case I found a way to get through.

The following afternoon a truck pulled up in front of Lidon's office. It was an empty truck of the Trans Sahara Company, bound for Gao. Lidon felt there was enough room for two other persons next to the driver. The French driver promised he would look after his human freight, although they wouldn't be able to understand one another.

"Goodbye, Dick. Goodbye, Dan."

"Goodbye, Dutchy."

The farewells were abrupt. "Good luck, boys." Yes, they deserved to get through. They were real friends.

Dick got in first and sat next to the driver. Dan followed. He opened the window and tears welled in his eyes. I wanted to say something but couldn't. The truck started moving. Dan waved a final goodbye and suddenly burst into tears. Forty-year-old Dan cried like a child.

The truck swayed over the square, picking up speed. Soon, after passing under the gateway of Adrar, en route to the southern horizon, my friends were out of sight. A cloud of dust remained, hanging around and trailing behind the truck until it was gone.

Some nerve-wracking days lay in store for me. At any moment, government officials or the Foreign Legion could pick me up and send me back to Europe. I had to fight resentment and hatred every time my thoughts touched on the happenings of the last few months. If the authorities would only *do* something. Anything. Then I would know where I stood. But no one knew anything or could do anything, and the oppressing uncertainty remained.

"There might be a chance we haven't thought of before," Lidon said without much conviction. "What about sending the highest authority in the country a telegram, and just explain everything." He seemed sincere.

"You don't mean the government in Algiers?" I asked. "They would only make things worse."

"That's what you may think," he said. "Don't forget they are the ones who gave you your visa in the first place. After all, what the government decides is law. Even the Trans Sahara Company can't overrule government decisions."

With that, the good-hearted Frenchman drew up another telegram—this time a rather long one.

There was no question of sleeping during the nights that followed. I lay awake on the stone bench at the mission, hundreds of times shifting position, but no sleep, not even rest was possible.

All kinds of plans formed in my mind. If only I could escape. If only I could walk the fifteen-hundred-mile distance across the desert. When I looked at the empty places where Dan and Dick had lain, I clenched my fists and once even beat my head against the wall in desperation. Back?! Go back?! No. Never. Never! Never!

In exasperation my thoughts reached back to another time of great need in my life. I remembered the God who had heard me in the concentration camp two years before. *I haven't been too faithful to Him*, I thought. I had gone my own way without confiding much in Him. The little New Testament was hidden in my backpack, nearly untouched for months. Things of more importance had taken its place. I prayed once in a while, but it was more a matter of habit than a person-to-person communication.

I could never forget the magnitude of God's presence during my most needy days in Camp Siegburg. How wonderfully He had answered my prayers and given me more time to live. Now, I was in a very different situation, but just as desperate.

I saw clearly that prayer was the answer, and I began to pray a few simple words to the God who had listened to me before. "Lord God, only you know a way out. Everything depends on you. Help me to succeed, or to lose gracefully."

After that, I felt somewhat relieved.

The next morning, the captain of the Foreign Legion summoned me to his office once again. He started with words I had expected some days ago, "Monsieur Vandenberg, you have now been here for three weeks. Mind you, three weeks without permission. Now, the Legion is fed up with keeping you here any longer. Again, I have received an order pertaining to you. That order is similar to the first one. Somehow you saw fit to miss the truck which was supposed to take you back two days ago; but this time I *must* send you back north—by force, if necessary."

Waiting a few seconds, he continued in a friendlier tone, "And seeing that you haven't found a way to get out of this oasis on your own . . ."

He didn't say the rest of what was on his mind. He only looked at me. After releasing a long sigh, he went on more sympathetically, "Tomorrow the colonel in charge of this region is due in Adrar for an inspection. He is the man who really runs the show in this part of the Sahara. Why don't you try to make an appointment with him? Perhaps you can throw more light on your case than I can. One never knows, young man."

With that, our conversation ended.

I turned on my heels with another faint hope in my heart.

A deep golden sun announced the arrival of another day. It didn't take long for the sky to begin vibrating before my eyes, the heat was so intense. A crowd of Arabs gathered on the square in front of the barracks of the Foreign Legion. They had come to add luster to the arrival of the colonel.

In the afternoon, a convoy of jeeps and army trucks of the Legion drove up, accompanied by a fantastic cloud of dust. The colonel rode in front and from his jeep flew the proud tricolor of France.

When a short official reception was over, from somewhere on the huge square in the midst of the Arab crowd came a soft beat of drums. Rapidly, the rhythm and volume increased, and the masses of Arab spectators started moving in the direction of the drums.

I watched a group of middle-aged Muslims in wide, striped robes form a circle. Near the heavy drums they shuffled in a long file behind one another, slowly tightening the circle around the drummers. The Arabs held their rifles pressed to their chests. Most of their guns were muzzle-loaders that must have served them during the desert wars against the French. The barrels of the rifles were pointed to the hard blue sky above.

Clouds of dust whirled around the stamping Arabs, but they didn't mind; they even seemed to like it. The faster the roll of the drums, the tighter the men thronged together. At last, the circle became a compact mass of sweating human bodies.

Suddenly the drummers jumped out of the circle of stamping Arabs and continued an even faster beat. The throb of the drums increased by the minute. The entire square disappeared under tremendous clouds of dust, and with shrill screeching the men in wide burnooses whipped themselves into a frenzy. When the tumult was at its peak, the Arabs fired their prehistoric guns in the air and the acrid smell of gunpowder and smoke mixed with the dust.

I tried to get out of the crowd of excited men to keep an eye on the colonel, but he had already retreated into the barracks of the Legion. The sentries at the gate didn't want to let me through. For a while I tried to convince the guards that I had an important message to convey, but my efforts were in vain.

When the last Arab finally left the square and the dust returned to earth, I retired to the cold, thick walls of the White Fathers' foyer.

Next morning I was permitted to see the colonel. That was an accomplishment; but I had little faith in just another meaningless talk. I preferred to tell him what I thought of the whole French bureaucracy. I was tired of sleepless nights, exhausted by roaming around and by these so-called interviews which always came to nothing. Everything and everyone got on my nerves. If I could only spit my venom in someone's face. An infuriating rage dominated my thoughts.

I had to wait some time in a hallway. In another corner stood an Arab who pulled with long strokes at a rope, the same way the church bells were rung in my hometown. Only here, there was no sound of ringing bells. The rope the Arab manipulated ran straight up toward the ceiling, turned over a pulley and disappeared through a hole in the wall to the adjoining room.

The riddle was solved when the door opened and I peeked inside. The colonel sat behind a large desk, and directly over him an enormous single-blade fan moved slowly from one side to the other. The rope was attached to the fan. Simple as it was, this apparatus worked efficiently, protecting Monsieur le Colonel against the harsh desert heat.

When I was ushered in, the colonel brushed some official papers aside and looked at me appraisingly. A single row of ribbons decorated his chest. His graying, stubby hair showed the imprint of his kepi and his face was strong, weather-beaten, and stern. He broke the silence. "What is your name again?" His voice was harsh and abrasive, the words issuing like a command, not a question.

"I am André Vandenberg."

He peered more closely at me. "So this is Vandenberg, eh? The individual who is causing us these never-ending problems." Folding his hands over his protruding stomach, he leaned back in his chair and appraised me from head to foot, his eyes glinting with disapproval.

"Would you tell me what kind of trouble, sir?" I began. "It seemed to me that paralyzing my movements could hardly have been a major problem for the Foreign Legion."

"Well, what are you doing here in military territory without a visa and without money?" he asked smugly.

I pulled my passport from my pocket, dug out the pile of banknotes from Mustafa, and threw them on the desk. "To start off, here is my passport," I said, "with a valid visa for the Sahara, issued by the Algerian government. This money is ample to complete my transit through the rest of the desert." I caught myself almost shouting, so glad was I to be able to nullify his allegations.

The colonel seemed taken aback. He picked up my passport and thumbed through the pages. Apparently he found things in order, for he glanced at me again, cast an eye on the money, and said, "It seems everything is in order."

He hesitated for a moment as if pondering the world's problems, then said, "As far as I am concerned, get out of here."

"Monsieur le Colonel," I said jubilantly, "just write those words on a piece of paper. It will help me convince the Trans Sahara Company that they have to take me across."

The officer hesitated a moment, pensively scratching his thinning hair. Then methodically he started jotting a few lines on a writing pad. He finally handed me the piece of paper on which I deciphered the following words: "As far as I can see, Mr. Vandenberg can continue his desert crossing. I have found his papers to be in order." An illegible signature confirmed the statement. I had passed inspection!

"Merci, merci beaucoup, Monsieur le Colonel. Mille fois, merci." I kept thanking him while I folded the valuable note and put my passport and money back in my pockets. With everything tucked away, I turned and headed for the door. I wanted out of the barracks before the colonel had a chance to change his mind.

A new courage surged through me. The Foreign Legion at least was not disposed to send me back. Half my battle was won.

Exultant over this first happy break in a month-long saga of disappointments, I marched to Lidon's office. As I neared, I saw him standing in his doorway. Coming closer, I saw that he was waving an envelope at me. He began to shout. "Monsieur, felicitations. This is a government wire for you."

Seconds later, I stood beside him, virtually tearing the envelope out of his hands. My eyes turned moist and began to blink when I read the paper inside: *For Heaven's Sake, Let That Dutchman Go*.

In a seven-ton truck loaded with cigarettes and tobacco, I left Adrar at last, heading south. I threw a last glance at Lidon, who after having given the driver his final instructions, stood back to wave his final goodbye.

In front of us shimmered a country of ill fame, the Tanezrouft, Land of Thirst. Somewhere in the heart of this awesome desert, Dan and Dick were fighting the sand, hard on the heels of Castor.

The cab of the truck was too small for three men; but the man next to me, the driver's helper, shifted position to allow me a bit of elbow room. This helper was an Arab named Ali. The driver was a Spaniard who called himself Sanchez. Ali and I occupied the right-hand corner of the cab, each of us perched on a wooden box. Between us and Sanchez was the head of the built-in engine.

We left Adrar in the middle of the day, and between the fierce sun above and the red-hot engine at our side, I felt more like a slow-frying chicken than a world traveler. But heat or no heat, I was on top of the world. I was free again, finally on my way south to the goal of South Africa. My next step was to try to catch up with Dan and Dick.

Toward evening we reached Reggan, the last oasis. There would be no more palms or wells, only endless stretches of sand. There was a transmitting station and a small hotel, both belonging to the Trans Sahara Company, and a few small, white buildings in Reggan. Only four Europeans lived there—the manager of the hotel, his wife, and two wireless operators.

The manager stood at the entrance of the hotel, awaiting our arrival. Our dust trail on the horizon had announced us.

As soon as greetings were exchanged, the manager's wife showed me to a room. I followed her, protesting that I could not afford any luxury and that I would be quite content to sleep in the cab of the truck. She simply waved off my objection as preposterous.

"I'm not interested in your money," she said. "I only want you to sleep comfortably. You've still got the roughest part ahead and this will be the last bed you'll spend the night on for quite some time."

When I took a dry crust of bread and some dates out of my backpack, this hospitable woman overruled me again. "Now stop this nonsense," she cried. "Keep your rations for later. We knew you were coming so we counted on your having dinner with us. The Trans Sahara Company can afford it." She told me to wash up and then join the others at the table.

So I ate and slept that night at the expense of that powerful company. It was as if the friendly people at this outpost of civilization wanted to make up for the hardships I had suffered.

As I lay on my comfortable bed, it came to me that in spite of every miserable thing that had happened, I had fallen in love with North Africa—or was it the case of a desolate spirit finding solace in a matching, woebegone landscape?

At five in the morning we left Reggan. It was still dark and chilly. Sanchez put on a woolen sweater and Ali and I drew closer together and warmed ourselves over the engine. The lights of the truck danced on the immeasurable plain. There was no more path. We were nearing the heart of the Sahara.

Sanchez stared intently ahead, following the tire marks other vehicles had left behind. At regular distances white-washed drums came into view, usually marked with numbers that represented the distance in kilometers to Gao in West Africa.

Abruptly, the sun rose over the eastern horizon and the desert changed into varying tints of soft amber. Soon we began to feel warm, and not long after that, hot.

Toward nine o'clock, a black dot became visible in the distance. The dot looked as if it had suddenly come out of the ground miles away. Sanchez, who had been watching the object for some time, remarked, "That truck. It's still there. I passed there more than a month ago. It had a broken axle, but the driver wasn't worried. He expected help any day."

Sanchez stared fixedly at it. "If it's the same truck, it belongs to a company that operates from West Africa. If that outfit only used road-worthy vehicles, it could save lots of time and money."

He squinted as we drew closer. "It's the same truck," he said. "Caramba!"

We stopped alongside the truck and got out. Immediately, the old truck came to life. The head of a black African appeared above the lowered window. The door opened and he jumped out. Another black man crawled out from between the front wheels. Both wore worn-out trousers and shabby, grease-streaked shirts.

"Still got enough to drink?" Sanchez asked.

"Oui, Monsieur."

"And what about food?"

The blacks replied that they had all the food they needed.

As the conversation went on, they said they were still waiting for the new axle shaft. A friendly driver had ordered one some weeks ago in Colomb-Bechar. One of these days another helpful driver would come along and drop it off.

No, they were not worried. They had full confidence in this tentative arrangement. Meanwhile, every passing vehicle stopped and provided any food or drink they might need. The grins on their faces showed no anxiety.

I looked around. A dreary desert of sand and pebbles stretched all the way to the horizon. No sign of life, nothing. It was an empty, silent, completely dead expanse wherever one looked. My respect grew for these two brave men.

Sanchez garnered information about the few persons and vehicles that had passed during the last several weeks. When he had satisfied his curiosity, we climbed back into the truck and drove on. Half an hour later the truck with the broken axle had vanished far behind us.

As the hours went by, the sand became looser. The driver perspired like a racehorse but never complained. An occasional "Caramba!" slipped from his lips whenever the truck labored through an extra loose patch.

We drove all day, wrestling with the sand. Low sand hills often blocked the tire marks. More and more often Sanchez shifted into four-wheel drive to get through the treacherous patches. The evening took the sting out of the sun, but Sanchez showed no signs of giving up his battle with the sand.

"We have to make Bidon Five tonight," he said. "Then we'll have done enough for the day." After a short interval he remarked, without looking in my direction, "We also have to try to lay our hands on this Castor, don't we?"

"The quicker the better," I said. "Let's get on with the job."

Twilight lasted only a short while. Suddenly we were enveloped in darkness. Countless tire marks were visible in the beams of the headlights. I couldn't make out which one the Spaniard followed. It looked as if the sand had been ploughed in all directions.

A sudden jolt snapped our heads forward, and we stopped. Sanchez pushed down the accelerator once more, but we didn't gain an inch. The wheels spun but we didn't move. We were stuck. He switched off the engine, threw the door open, and jumped into the sand. Ali and I followed.

"Not too bad yet," Sanchez mumbled when he had studied the position of the back wheels, "let's try to dig out of here. Remember, leave the front wheels alone. Only dig away the sand directly in front of the back tires." He fell on his knees and started digging sand with his hands.

Ali and I cleaned away the sand on the other side, and within ten minutes the four back tires were free. Ali pulled two fifteen-foot poles from under the truck and wedged them between the double wheels.

When Sanchez was assured that the poles were in the right places, he climbed behind the wheel and started the engine. Slowly the heavy truck vibrated forward, the back wheels slid onto the poles, and the truck moved. At the end of the poles it stopped again. For a moment the wheels spun, then they sank deeper in the loose sand.

Again we dug away the sand and shoved the poles into position, and once more Sanchez inched the truck forward. This time the vehicle zigzagged about thirty yards through the troublesome sand. Ali and I took one of the poles each, dragged them behind us and followed the truck. Again the sand won against the powerful engine, for after a few heavy shudders the Renault stopped and the back wheels dug their graves once more.

Stubbornly we fought on, digging sand with our hands and dragging the poles through the furrows the truck left behind. After many short bursts, the truck finally came to rest with the wheels dug deeply into the sand.

"Men," Sanchez said, "we'd better capitulate. This is no use. We have arrived at exactly the same spot where I had to dig out eighty times on my last crossing."

He looked around, kicked viciously into a heap of sand, and then put his hands in his pockets.

Ali had no comment. The Arab probably recognized Sanchez as his superior in the realm of sand. Of course, Ali was a fatalistic Arab who could easily adjust to all kinds of unpleasant circumstances.

"If we wait till tomorrow," the Spaniard predicted, "the sand will be somewhat harder. Then at least we'll be able to see what we're doing. So let's call it a day. How about some solid food for a change?"

Sanchez knelt in the sand and dug an oblong hole. When it was sufficiently deep, Ali uncovered some wood from the load and lit a fire. Soon a crackling campfire brightened our evening.

Within half an hour, Sanchez had fixed a good stew of potatoes, onions, meat, and macaroni. Not a word was spoken while we worked down our dinner. Sanchez became communicative again when Ali began brewing Arab coffee. The three of us lay around the sandpit staring into the flames.

When the coffee was finished, Sanchez stretched himself lazily and announced, "I'm going to hit the sack."

Climbing into the cabin of the truck, he fumbled in the dark and found a roll of old cloth which he spread over the engine. This was his bed. The engine kept its warmth for quite a while and Sanchez made the most of it. The desert air became rather chilly and even the sand cooled fast.

Ali spread the embers of the fire over the bottom of the pit and threw handfuls of sand on it to put out the fire. "This my bed," he announced. "Nice and warm."

He covered himself with his robes, and I had to agree that he had not chosen the worst part in this lonely desert. The sands beneath him would stay warm for a long while. And if a cold wind came up and swept over the plains, it would blow right over his hole in the ground.

I was not sleepy. I was too anxious about our predicament to relax, and decided to walk instead. Above was a starry sky of an astounding magnificence. Enormous stars glowed in gorgeous splendor. The sight fascinated me. Although the night was moonless, I could see for miles. At a considerable distance, I spotted a wreck of a car gleaming in the light of the stars. The wreck was buried up to its hood in the sand. A little farther, I discovered the next wreck, another victim of the Sahara. The more I surveyed the area, the more vehicles, or parts thereof, I detected, all sticking partly out of the sand.

The temperature dropped fast and I began to get cold. Back at the truck I pulled out one of the mattresses we were to deliver to Bidon Five. For shelter I shoved the mattress behind one of the back tires, and exhausted, stretched out on top of it. Then I pulled my blanket high over my shoulders and tried to sleep. A vicious cold wind swept in from the east and made me shiver. Only when I laid a second mattress on top of me was I able to fall asleep.

Next afternoon we reached *Bidon* Five. Bidon is French for a large drum, and quite rightly this settlement was called "The Five Drums" for its five barracks, made out of corrugated iron and placed neatly in a row. Besides the iron huts, the French had built a transmitting station and a simple lookout post. Here we got sufficient water and oil for the next few days.

One Arab sergeant and two French soldiers managed this solitary post for six months a year. For half a year the three looked at one another and the few dried-up travelers who ventured a crossing of the Sahara. The other half of the year the outpost was abandoned; even the experienced Trans Sahara Company didn't risk crossing the desert during that period.

From one of the French soldiers I learned that Dan and Dick were three days ahead of us, and that Castor was two days ahead of them. Even though we had pursued them as fast as we could, we hadn't gained even half a day.

After Bidon Five, the desert changed slowly. In the east, mighty mountain peaks reached for the sky. These were the Hoggar Mountains, Sanchez said, one of the most desolate and inaccessible ranges on the globe. It was the heart of the Sahara, a region nearly the size of Europe. Between the clefts of these barren, rugged mountains lived the Berbers, free nomads who ignored the French domination of their area.

Once, Ali discovered a line of camels on the horizon. The riders were traders on ancient caravan routes. At that distance, they and their camels looked like tiny chess pieces arranging themselves for play.

The tracks of other vehicles sometimes disappeared altogether, for gradually black grit had taken the place of sand. The dunes around us became quite higher than they had been for the last few days, and every hour more boulders appeared. Even some lonely grass blades showed up in this desolate country. Little by little we were again nearing habitable regions.

As another day passed, the single grass blades gradually changed into grass patches. In some places there were even small bushes. Suddenly an antelope emerged from the rocks and bounded along in front of the truck. Sanchez became excited and pushed the accelerator to the floor, trying to run down the beautiful animal. But the antelope remained at a safe distance; then with an unpredictable leap, it bolted sideways and ran with the speed of an arrow along the vast plain.

More grass came into view, more bushes, and more antelope. Even a lonely, miniature tree dared a small attempt at life. After this first one, others followed. Sometimes a frightened hornbill flew up. Then for miles there would be nothing at all.

The trail of vehicle tracks slowly changed into a kind of narrow, sandy pathway; and when I discovered in the distance the first native huts, I realized that the second important phase of my journey to South Africa lay behind me. The European and Arab worlds were in the past for me now. A new and fascinating world of black Africans lay ahead.

Small black boys clad only in loincloths ran out of the huts at the sound of our engine. They leaped and ran nearly as fast as the slender antelope we had passed. Spontaneously, they waved at us. I wondered what these people existed on in this inhospitable area. Only about half the land was covered with thin grass. The other half consisted of sand and pebbles.

Once in a while we passed Tuaregs who looked down on us like princes from their camels. They were somewhat darker than the Arabs, and they appeared at least as proud. The Tuaregs were in a strange way still the masters of this part of the desert. They wore long, blue burnooses and turbans of the same color. For protection against the smarting sand, they had part of their turbans pulled in front of their faces. Only their eyes were unhidden.

Actually, they formed the only existing tribe of veiled men. Strangely, Tuareg women do not wear veils. According to many Europeans acquainted with this area, the Tuaregs still use the black inhabitants of this country as bond servants, be it in some mild form. The French overlords were unable to do much about it, and therefore had to condone the situation.

Large herds of well-fed Zebu cattle walked sullenly past. Droves of donkeys, looking in much better shape than those in North Africa, idled lazily behind the herds. Black Africans worked as cowboys.

Suddenly, the rocky plateau on which we drove came to an end and became a rather steep decline. Sanchez drove slowly, taking carefully the hairpin turns that led to the lower regions before us.

Looking past Ali's head, I saw to our left an unbelievable panorama. At the end of the decline, a wide river flowed majestically. Reeds in the river and grass along the banks were as fresh as the green pastures of my native Holland. The bright blue water of the river mirrored trees on its banks.

"Is this the Niger?" I asked Sanchez.

"Yes, that's the Niger, all right. The third largest river in Africa. Only the Congo and the Nile are bigger." Sanchez spoke as proudly as if he himself were the discoverer. "This river is over two thousand miles long. You haven't got anything mightier in all Europe. Can you imagine? A river like this flowing right through the desert!"

For me, the desert ended with the emergence of this enormous river. I was elated. I was winning my personal challenge of the African continent.

Chapter Eight

SURPRISES ALONG
THE NIGER

A young woman of the Songhai tribe, draped in gaily colored cloth, squatted on the river bank washing the hollowed out gourds they used for dishes. Fifty feet off the bank, a man slid past in a dugout canoe. He paddled idly, as if he had all the time in the world. At intervals he shouted something to the woman. She answered and both laughed. The water rippled along the bank. Rows of rice plants in shallow water bent the tops of their stems as the weak current flowed by.

The woman finished her dishes and stacked all the gourds one on top of the other. She then placed the pile skillfully on her head and walked with a natural grace along the narrow path following the river. Swaying her hips a little, she disappeared around a bend of the little road.

My eyes roamed over the high reeds and clear water and I felt happier than I had in a long time. It was only eight in the morning and not really hot yet. We had just arrived at Bourem, the first village of any importance south of the Tanezrouft. Few Europeans lived in Bourem, but they occupied nice houses and had green shrubs in their gardens. All their window openings were covered with fine screen, which gave the houses the look of being block huts without any real openings.

Our delay in Bourem was to be about three hours. Sanchez had to send a wire to the Trans Sahara Company in Colomb-Bechar to report the safe arrival of truck and cargo. No mention was made of the Dutchman.

A little before noon we continued our trip south. The road followed the course of the Niger. Along the river were waving reeds, green grass, and some small trees, but about two hundred yards away from the river, the desert prevailed. High, naked sand dunes stood along the path on our left. Green-yellow beach grass survived in patches along the road. Now and again, brush ventured life on the slopes of the dunes.

Ali dozed off and Sanchez himself had difficulty keeping his eyes open. After about three hours the first houses of Gao appeared on the horizon. At last the truck stopped in front of the little tropical hotel of the Trans Sahara Company. My crossing of the Sahara had ended.

A European in khaki shorts greeted Sanchez. At once the two started bragging about personal achievements. Ali left the cab and silently disappeared.

As soon as I climbed out, I saw a man in a sergeant's uniform like those worn by the French police. He came toward me as I walked around the truck to get my backpack. Politely he said, "Excuse me, Monsieur, aren't you the friend of the two Englishmen?"

Instinctively I smelled danger. I had only touched the soil of this next country, and the police already had wind of it. To gain time and not jeopardize my position, I asked innocently, "About what Englishmen are you talking, Monsieur?"

Without taking his eyes off me, he said, "About three days ago two Englishmen arrived here in Gao. Unfortunately, I found out a little too late that they traveled without any means to support themselves. I am certain that you are aware that one of the conditions to enter this colony is being in possession of a certain amount of cash in order not to become a burden to the state."

He hesitated a moment and then went on, "By chance it has come to my attention that these two Englishmen had another friend who was also on his way to Gao. Are you this person, or aren't you?"

A smouldering fire deep inside me flared up. This *had* to be a land mine laid by Castor, this notification of authorities along the way that we were broke, to make sure that Dan, Dick, and I would never reach British territory.

I tried to control my feelings in the presence of the sergeant, for I was not yet sure how dangerous he could be to me. Avoiding a direct answer, I asked instead, "Now if these two Englishmen were friends of mine, what could I do about their financial status?"

"That's just the point," he answered quickly. "Because these two Englishmen have no means of support here in West Africa, I assume that you might be in the same unfortunate position. That's why I am here, to check how you are faring financially."

I assured him without much conviction that my personal finances were in perfect order. (Couldn't I add up my entire fortune on the fingers of one hand!)

Sanchez came to my rescue. He caught sight of the sergeant talking to me and quickly walked over to greet him. Approaching the sergeant from behind, he acted as if he recognized a long-lost brother, hollering in French, "Hi there, my dear Doumergue. How are you, old man?"

The two embraced like lovers. Then they started a lively conversation and I was sure this would be followed by a few drinks for old time's sake.

While Sanchez and the sergeant bantered, I walked cautiously to the back of the truck, climbed in between the tobacco and cigarettes, and uncovered my backpack. I had to get out of here quickly. I didn't fancy another long delay. So I started walking to the native town I had seen in the distance, making sure I kept the truck between the zealous sergeant and myself. I kept going as fast as I could, trying to figure out my next move.

I knew at least one person in Gao who would be able to help me in case of emergency—Mustafa Saada, my benefactor of Adrar days! Besides, I had the names of the White Fathers in this town. If I somehow could make it to either of these two addresses undetected, there was a reasonable chance to stay out of the hands of the police.

The more distance I put between the sergeant and me, the quieter my heartbeat became. I had noticed thousands of small mud houses lying in the valley a few miles away. They appeared to be scattered at random without plan or design.

Adjoining the large native city was the European quarter, not of the most charming style either. I had expected something much more picturesque of my first West African town.

After about an hour, I reached the first native houses. Though it was past siesta time, it was still quiet in the huge area where numberless tribal people were crowded together in brown, ugly mud houses. Now and again, I met an African in ravelled pants. Half-naked kids played in the unpaved, smelly alleys.

The houses were made of clay and had no architectural beauty whatever. In most cases the roofs were flat. As in the Arab world, windows were virtually unknown. A few holes in the earthen walls were the only openings to provide fresh air, light, and ventilation. A heavy odor of food and grease hung in the air. The sweltering heat made me perspire badly.

Fortunately, the first man I spoke to was able to tell me in poor French where Mustafa lived. Soon I stood in front of a heavy wooden door in a low wall. I knocked hard and loud, and didn't have to wait long. The studded door opened with a long, drawn-out creak, and the face of a black man appeared in the opening.

"Does Monsieur Mustafa Saada live here?"

The round face nodded and disappeared again. A few seconds later he was back and invited me in with a broad grin. "Come in, sir. This way." When I stepped inside, he bowed graciously, then led the way through a dark passage.

My eyes had to get used to the dark, but the coolness of the passage felt good. The low wall I had been looking at from the street was actually the back wall of a long row of adjoining rooms, all built in a square around the main building, which stood a little ways back in the center of a courtyard. I guessed these rooms were Mustafa's servants' quarters. The house in the center had some vague resemblance to Arab architecture, with windows high enough to be out of reach.

My guide pushed aside several long rows of beads which covered the door opening. The room before me was furnished in Arab style. Three coffee tables stood in various parts of the room and on one of these hand-carved tables stood a silver tea service. Heavy oriental cushions were spread around the low tables. Against one of these cushions, legs crossed under him, sat Mustafa.

"So, it is you, the Dutchman," he said, showing no emotion, but he did get up and walk toward me. With Arab dignity he made the gracious welcome signs, touching with his three largest fingers his eyes, his lips, and his heart, meaning that these now belonged to his guest. Then he pointed to one of the fancy cushions and indicated that I should make myself comfortable.

In a few words, I summarized the events that had taken place since we last met in the grocery shop of Adrar. I didn't leave out the part of my encounter with the local sergeant.

At that, Mustafa frowned. Slowly he shook his head and remarked with a shade of sarcasm, "Life certainly was not meant to be easy for you."

I nodded in total agreement.

"But I wouldn't worry about it," he said, stroking his beard. "We'll find a way out."

Curious to know what had happened to my English friends, I switched the conversation to Dan and Dick and asked whether he knew what had become of them.

"Your friends are still going in the right direction," he said with a smile. "They passed by here, too, but most of their time in Gao was spent at the Mission of the White Fathers. They left the day before yesterday with an acquaintance of mine who went on a trip south. So don't have any concern about them. They're still enjoying freedom."

After a moment he added, "I admire those men. They don't know a word of any language spoken within a thousand miles, but they're finding their way just the same."

The man who had opened the front door for me brought in some tea. Mustafa kept quiet and waited till we were alone again before he stirred the tea, then poured it into small glasses on the silver tray.

"What kind of idea did you get of Castor during your crossing?" I asked. "You traveled together on the same Trans Sahara bus, so you were able to watch him very closely."

"I must say, he acted like a gentleman," Mustafa said. "It is hard to imagine that this man has on his conscience the type of crimes you have told me he committed."

"If someone had told me a similar story about Castor when I met him," I said, "I wouldn't have believed it either. I had to go through a lot of hardships at his hands before I finally dropped out of his entourage."

"He was kind of—how should I say?" Mustafa tried to explain his observations of Castor, "Well, the best expression would be, kind of nervous now and again. But that is really all that came to my attention."

"Do you think I have a chance of catching up with him?" I asked.

Mustafa looked at me closely. "That wouldn't be easy. By now he is a week ahead of you. The four of them took off for Naimey as fast as they could, I believe with another bus of the Trans Sahara Company. You'd better watch every step you take. Keep in mind that your former chief has many advantages over you. I am certain that he still has some money left from that truck—I believe he called it the *Desert Rat*. He sold it in Geryville for a nice amount of cash. We both know you haven't got a penny, so forget about trying to find him. You'd be better off saving your own skin instead of thinking of revenge."

I sighed, but knew Mustafa was right.

After moments of silence, the Arab surprised me with an unexpected suggestion. "Since you have nothing better to do but hide from the police, you may as well stay around here for awhile. We can enjoy dinner together, and after dark you can call on the White Fathers and spend the night there."

What hiding place could be better than the sanctuary of this Arab mogul? Mustafa surely had a bigger heart than his austere features suggested. He might be a man with different principles and eccentric tastes. He might follow unusual and even revolting customs; but in my memory he will forever stand out as a dignified Muslim benefactor. Devoid of selfish motives, he had assisted us in Adrar; and now, once again, Mustafa came up with a solution to my problem.

Totally broke in a land where the white man had to keep up his image as master, and fearing repercussions by the local authorities because of it, I spent hours on the embroidered cushions of Mustafa's lounge. Then, after a long tea-sipping session one afternoon, he casually said, "I happen to know a man who is quite willing to take you farther along to the south."

Mustafa probably had known this all along, but in perfect restraint he chose to wait for the right moment.

"This friend of mine is Monsieur Banton," he said. "He intends to leave for Naimey tomorrow morning. If you're interested in going with him, you will be able to find him tonight in the bar La Douce France."

Early in the evening, I headed for the bar. There near the front door were two Frenchmen enjoying their favorite drink, anisette. One was Mustafa's friend Banton. He was a trader who went from native village to native village, buying and selling all kinds of animal skins and crops.

Banton's companion was an ex-colonial army officer who had spent most of his adulthood in tropical Africa. Going by the name "Pinard," the name of a sour French army wine, he had chosen to spend his retirement in the wilds of Africa rather than in civilized France. On this occasion, he had joined Banton, hoping to run into some excitement. Neither man had shaved for days, nor from the smell and dirt on their khaki outfits, did it seem they had changed clothes during that time. But their sunburnt faces showed expressions of interest in my plight. These expressions proved genuine. They offered me a free ride all the way to Naimey in the back of their truck.

During the days that followed, the men divided their tasks. Banton usually entertained himself with business, bartering with the natives in villages along the road. Pinard provided the necessary meat. No animal within range of his rifle was safe.

One day we were told that large game was more plentiful on the opposite bank of the Niger. Pinard decided to investigate and invited me to come along. He recruited a two-man crew from the Songhai village where we had passed the night. At the local landing site for dugouts, we were faced with the decision of which craft would be the most river-worthy. After a half-hour of excited bargaining, Pinard and the locals came to an agreement. The crowd started yelling with delight as two muscular natives took up their places in the vessel. Pinard and I followed with considerably less agility than the experienced Africans.

For the first half-mile, we were closed in by giant reeds; the oarsmen pushed us through a labyrinth of humid tunnels which previous canoes had plowed open. But finally the ten-foot tall stalks gave way to the open river.

Our dugout canoe glided gracefully downstream. It was amazing to see how skillfully the two Africans navigated the hollowed-out log. The Niger River was about three miles wide at this point, and we kept a course in the center of the stream. One man stood in the front of the canoe, expertly manipulating a long, hand-carved oar. A few strokes on one side, a few on the other, and the dugout slid ahead without the slightest roll.

The man behind us steered the craft, using a short oar. He was also the song leader. While keeping on course, he worked through a repertoire of lyrics. The moment his deep voice boomed another melody, his companion in the bow joined him, and another African tune rolled over the blue waters.

For a long distance, the Niger was as languid as the night, serene and placid. However, after a spell of tranquility, the boatmen abruptly stopped singing. The one in front sat down and concentrated on something ahead. I saw no indication of anything out of the ordinary except a few extra ripples on either side of the dugout. But the Africans saw something else. They held their oars out of the water and waited.

The sound of rushing water became audible. No longer sulky and brooding, the majestic Niger leaped into sudden violence.

I expected our navigators to steer immediately for one of the banks, but they didn't. They just sat there, tense and ready, oars in hand, staring at the fast-approaching rocks ahead.

The dugout began to race at an alarming speed. I held on to both sides, terrified. Clouds of spray surrounded us, and careening crazily on white-frosted water we shot past an overhanging boulder. Between a row of high, black rocks I could see the water ahead rushing downward into an abyss. As if steered by an unseen hand, the native craft slipped into this darker, faster water. Nothing could stop us now. We were hurled into a gaping four-foot opening between two boxcar-sized rock formations. I wished these oarsmen would do something. Anything! But the man in front remained rigid, holding his oar in such a grip that the muscles on his arms flexed like ropes. I didn't dare look back at what number two was doing.

With a swift sweep, the dugout tilted a bit and we surfed through the first cataract, barely missing a murderous black rock which hurdled past less than a foot away.

The moment the dugout brushed past the first rock, the natives paddled frantically to keep it in the current. I felt the water moving faster once more and we slipped through another seething, roaring passage. The side of the canoe scraped slightly over the face of a protruding rock. To my amazement, the dugout remained flat on her keel while flashing past new obstacles.

As suddenly as they had showed up, the cataracts disappeared, and we floated again on quiet water. The crew dipped their oars in the clear surface as if nothing had happened. When the man on the bow got up again, I understood there would be no more rapids for a while. With renewed vigor, the men resumed their singing. Their deep voices boomed out the ages-old African songs as we glided down the tranquil river.

A long, narrow island loomed at the horizon, thick with bushes and trees. Pinard gave some instructions in the local dialect to our boat crew, and shortly the dugout swerved in the direction of the island. When we came close, Pinard informed me, "I have to see the native chief about the movement of big game around here."

The huts on the island were built on stilts, a precaution I had not observed before in villages along the river bank. Also on stilts were some peculiar-looking structures built in the form of large eggs and flattened on the top. I could detect neither window nor door in these odd ten-foot-tall shapes. Pinard explained that they were grain storehouses.

Dozens of islanders crowded the waterfront to stare at the unexpected visitors. At least half were naked, and others wore old rags as loincloths. Goats with bloated bellies ruminated near the silos and naked kids with protruding navels chased dwarf hens.

A black man of tremendous dimensions neared Pinard as we came ashore and greeted him in broken French, "My dear friend, very happy again to see you. How are you?" With these words this huge man, apparently the village chief, had lavished on Pinard his entire stock of French. From then on, he babbled in local dialect. Repeatedly he pointed toward the western bank of the Niger. He used both hands while talking excitedly, his eyes rolling in their sockets like brown marbles. Pinard nodded, probably drawing his own conclusions.

The chief then called two men, pointed at a large dugout and ordered them to get in. Pinard, the chief, and six other local men also climbed into the canoe. I boarded our own dugout again, and with the original crew at the oars we followed the larger one. An excited crowd yelled after us and throngs of naked kids ran along the shoreline until they came to the end of their muddy island.

Again we followed the Niger downstream. There weren't many reeds on the west bank, enabling us to keep a proper look-out over the interior. A row of hills about four miles inland broke the flat horizon.

The chief yelled something in our direction and the two canoes changed course and slid toward the bank. With a soft thud, the front point of our vessel rammed into the wet, black earth and stuck fast. The chief climbed out of his boat and lumbered up the bank, followed by all the others. That, however, was contrary to what Pinard had in mind. After some confusion and a lot of shouting, the Frenchman sent the large dugout canoe with its entire entourage, chief included, back to the island.

"If they had stayed with us," Pinard commented, "we couldn't catch a grasshopper. They were only to come along and show us where they had seen game in the past few days."

Our crewmen were the only ones Pinard allowed to remain with us. They tied our canoe to an overhanging tree.

"I don't want to hear a sound from any of you," Pinard warned. "Shut up, be on your guard, and keep your eyes open. I want to lay my hands on some sizeable game pretty fast."

We turned and strode toward the interior. We followed no path, and Pinard, who led the way, had to force a passage through the green undergrowth. A prickly weed, *krak-kram*, caught onto our clothing. This was real bush country.

A bird flew up, twittering shrilly, made a large circle over us, and alighted farther to the left. The sun, pleasantly warm half an hour before, had become blistering hot. Briars thickened, now lashing at our faces. Pinard pushed on, oblivious to everything but his goal. His sun helmet dangled on the back of his head and he munched a cigarette as if it were chewing tobacco.

An hour later, the bush began to open up and Pinard indicated that he wanted us to spread out in the form of a horseshoe. He took his rifle from the gun-bearer and slipped off the safety, readying it to fire instantly.

Another hour went by with nothing in view that resembled game. Then suddenly Pinard pointed at something peering from behind thick bushes—a family of monkeys. No, not monkeys, baboons; they had no hair on their behinds. The family kept a safe distance from us and watched closely as we passed.

"There!" The sweating Pinard tried to subdue a hoarse whisper, pointing toward a nearby hill. I stared in the same direction but saw nothing. My eyes were not yet accustomed to details obvious to this hunter. Pinard continued to lead the way, more cautious than before. With one raised finger and flashing his eyes, he gave us an extra warning to be careful and quiet.

Suddenly I saw movement. Straining my eyes, I detected a few animals which looked like pigs. The Frenchman moved on in the direction of the animals. We moved another two hundred yards and were able to distinguish the creatures much better. As I looked toward them, the heads of the entire group came up, their motion stopped, and they faced our way. Then they broke into a run, each with its tail straight up in the air, stampeding away from us.

117

Fast as the twinkling of an eye, Pinard brought his rifle to his shoulder, drew a swift bead, and fired. At the boom of his rifle, we raced behind the fleeing animals.

"Warthogs!" Pinard hollered, delightedly. "Warthog! Man, that's good eating!"

For a minute, I saw nothing but dust and swaying elephant grass. Then the Africans and I arrived at an open plain which the Frenchman had reached ahead of us.

With a sudden jerk, Pinard turned around and yelled, "Take cover!"

Thirty yards away, a massive, swine-like animal headed straight for us. Pinard had apparently failed to hit a vital spot, for the warthog was wounded only in the left front leg.

Snorting angrily, he charged us with all the speed remaining in his three good legs. Two dangerous tusks protruded from his jaws, and he looked as if he were saying, "If you want my life, you'll have to fight for it!"

He put all his rage in his charge, and probably because I was nearest, headed for me. Nearer he thundered as I looked frantically for something to climb. Twenty yards! Ten!

BOOM! Out of the corner of my eye, I saw Pinard, down on one knee, his rifle aimed, fire squirting from the barrel toward the wounded animal. With a heavy thud the warthog slammed to the ground just in front of me.

"Keep away from him!" Pinard shouted. "Don't get near! That rascal might be playing dead. He would tear you to pieces if he got a chance."

Pinard reloaded his rifle and kept it aimed at the mass of meat at my feet.

After a full minute, the animal hadn't budged. We circled around him. I counted the holes the shots had made and admired the yellowed tusks. Pinard debated aloud which pieces of meat were most suitable to take along. He pulled out a hunting knife and started skinning the animal.

"We'll take the hams and filets," Pinard said. "The rest is going to be too heavy. The hams alone will be sufficient to keep us alive till we reach Naimey." Systematically, he cut out these choice pieces.

Soon the once-colossal warthog was reduced to a bloody mess. So was the ground around it. Vultures hovered overhead, and while coming ever nearer, made circles smaller and smaller. The most daring ones landed near the butchery and stared at the remains with insolent eyes.

An hour later we were on our way back to the canoe.

Late in the afternoon, we arrived at our dugout. The oarsmen loosened it from the tree. Sweaty and bloodstained, they took their hand-carved paddles and headed immediately for the middle of the river. Pinard sat in front of me, contented, now and then commenting briefly on the successful hunt. I contemplated the hams and filets at my feet and appreciated the free food they represented.

Instead of keeping the dugout in the center of the river, the boatmen made straight for the other side, then followed the shoreline upstream.

Toward sunset we reached the cataracts. Rushing, turbulent waters were right ahead of us. The rays of the sun sent streaks of light over the low clouds of white spray, producing irregular patches of rainbow.

Our crew didn't tackle the cataract upstream but headed for a sandy bank where they unloaded the meat and pulled the dugout ashore. With our help, they lifted the craft on their shoulders and started with their heavy load along a pathway, following the river.

I shouldered the hams and followed them. Last in our short procession was the indomitable French hunter, who strung the filets over the barrel of his rifle and carried them on his shoulder. Ugly flies buzzed around my head and lighted on the meat, eager to get a share of the bounty. Clouds of mosquitoes joined them.

As soon as we bypassed the cataracts, we took to the water again. I felt drained and was happy to take my seat once more. Twilight faded at the western horizon and a balmy tropical evening settled on the Niger. Besides the splashing of the oars, untold mysterious voices floated on the air, composing the fascinating melody of the huge continent. I sat spellbound, listening to these captivating sounds. To me they represented the hidden soul of Africa.

Banton waited at a campfire, happy when we arrived with meat for supper. He instantly started roasting a large piece of filet. Pinard called the oarsmen and donated one of the hams for their services. Although Pinard and I were exhausted, we joined Banton in devouring most of the steak.

The dust behind the noisy truck curled and hovered like a smoke screen, obliterating French West Africa. We had just crossed the border into Nigeria and it would be only another two hundred miles to Kano and maybe even Dan and Dick . . . or Castor and company.

With relief I left French territory behind me. True, I had made some wonderful, unforgettable friends along the troublesome trail, but it seemed there were always authorities to block my way, to keep my dream of settling in South Africa from coming true. With arrival in Nigeria, the shadow of the French police melted into my past for good.

I had covered almost a thousand miles since leaving Banton and Pinard in Naimey. The long road had taken me past primitive native villages with mud-encrusted, naked kids; past women with fantastic hair styles, draped in faded cloth; along savanna fires of several miles width; and through country where peanut crops offered local people an income.

Since virtually all peanuts were shipped by truck to Kano in Nigeria, it had been easy to hitch a ride to the border and across it. I had secured a seat among a dozen malodorous natives on top of an overloaded peanut truck. They were pleasantly disposed, roaring with laughter and talking continuously.

It was finally evening and the driver switched on the headlights. They flickered for a moment, then went out, and the truck stopped. The driver emerged from the cab to check out the problem under the hood. As he worked, I watched the evening sky lose its afterglow. The jabbering of the Africans on the peanut sacks intensified, and soon a velvet night enveloped us.

The driver gave up. He shouted something to us and everybody on top of the truck moved about a little, stretching out the best they could. That apparently meant we would remain here through the night, so I followed the example of the others and folded up for some sleep on the lumpy sacks.

Within a short time, the Africans were snoring happily. Sometimes the snoring swelled as if it were a noisy hurricane. I wanted to take a walk, but didn't get off, afraid of losing my few square feet of sleeping space.

Thoughts of Dan and Dick ran through my mind and I wondered what had happened to them. Had they ever arrived in Kano? Would they still be there? Would Castor be waiting to cause more problems? What welcome would the British give me in their colony?

We were on our way at the crack of dawn, heading toward Kano and another hot day. After a rough, three-hour ride, a large town came into view. It was not a pretty town. Dirt-colored huts and mud hovels were haphazardly thrown together, tens of thousands of them. They made up the vast native quarter of Kano, a district said to contain more than two hundred-fifty thousand souls. Over this miserable squalor, two white and slender minarets of the local mosque rose high in the blue sky.

Vultures flew in wide circles above the town. Now and then, one dove into the brown mass of dirt houses, presumably performing its mission as Kano's sanitation department. In places like this, where sewers and trash collectors were unknown, the services of vultures were well nigh indispensable. As we drew nearer, I could see an enormous earthen wall around this native quarter, separating it from more affluent areas.

When the truck stopped, my fellow riders climbed noisily off and soon were lost in the surging crowd of men and women wearing long white robes. Ten minutes later, the driver cleared the walled city and moved into a less poverty-stricken part of town. When he stopped the truck again, I knew it was my turn to depart and find my own way. I climbed off and thanked him.

Now to track down Dan and Dick. After inquiring for several hours, I found that the government had made available a number of houses in the suburb of Bompai for the benefit of people who were stranded in Kano. A young Englishman offered to drive me there.

Toward noon we reached Bompai, and though dirty, tired, and hungry, I felt completely joyous—and with good reason. The truck stopped in front of a neat-looking bungalow. The front door was ajar, and when the driver sounded his horn, a man appeared in the door opening. It took me a moment to recognize Dan. His well-rounded torso had disappeared and a lean person with a thin face looked at me.

His mouth opened slowly. Then, in simulated Italian, Dan's voice shouted, "Amico Mio! My friend! My friend!"

On the spur of the moment, we embraced one another as only a couple of real Frenchmen should be able to do!

Chapter Nine

ENCOUNTERS ON THE EQUATOR

"Sit down and make yourself comfortable," said the young Englishman, pointing to a wooden crate.

I looked around the room. A smoking candle attempted to light a messy, smelly living room full of camping equipment. My eyes dwelt enviously on various pots and pans, a Coleman stove, and a pile of mosquito netting. Not a single picture decorated the yellow walls, dirty and badly scratched. Meanwhile, two Englishmen blew smoke from their cigarettes toward the quivering flame, at times nearly extinguishing it.

Dan had informed me that one of these men had tried to contact me, but he didn't know why. Now, sitting motionless on the wooden crate, I wondered, too, but didn't ask, thinking it wiser to let them make the first move.

"You tell him, Bill," said the younger of the two. In no hurry, Bill flipped his cigarette butt to the floor and ground it into dust with the toe of his shoe.

Bill was tallest of the two, a good-looking, well-built young man clad in clean, starched khaki shorts and safari shirt.

"I came to see you this afternoon," Bill said, "to ask if you would like to join us. We are planning to go to Nairobi in Kenya. Mind you, I said 'planning.' As you well know, nothing can be taken for granted in Africa. Frank and I both were recently discharged from the British army, so we have no money. However, we do offer other advantages. We have access to a lorry which we must take to the owner in Nairobi. We also have some old clothes, cigarettes, and soap which we intend to swap with the natives for food.

"Our biggest problem," he added, "is that we lack papers."

He stopped abruptly there, waiting for the effect of his last statement. Then he began again: "We have no visas for French Equatorial Africa or the Belgian Congo, and I'm sure such papers are unobtainable here in Kano. So we've decided to take a chance and go without them. There is another Englishman by the name of Robert who wants to join us; so if we put our coins and heads together we can make it till either our luck or the petrol runs out."

He paused again for effect, then quietly offered: "How about taking the chance with us?"

Silently, I digested the proposition. According to the British immigration officer in Kano, I had already overstayed my welcome. My not being a British subject meant I was flirting with deportation.

Old, faithful Dan had made up his mind to stay in Kano for a while, mainly to recuperate from the travails of the past months. Besides, he was an Englishman by birth, and had a local bank account.

Dick had decided to report to the police and take deportation. "I've seen enough of this continent," he said, "and I'd rather be deported back to good old England at the expense of the taxpayer."

That left me on my own again, and I harbored no thoughts of going back. But I wanted to be extremely careful. I wanted to avoid any repetition of my problems crossing the Sahara. Still, this trip to Nairobi would bring me three thousand miles closer to my destination.

"There is something Bill didn't mention," Frank interrupted my thoughts. "If you decided to try your luck with us, that's up to you, but that doesn't mean we guarantee you a safe arrival in Kenya. We pool the money we have and we'll make a go of it. In case we get stranded somewhere in the jungle because of breakdown, lack of money, or maybe police interference, that will mean the end of the journey.

"I guess what I'm trying to say," he concluded, "is that this trip is not like a marriage contract. It's 'for better or you're on your own.'"

At least these guys seem honest, I reassured myself, wary of another Castor-type expedition. But no one had talked about the actual cost.

"What's this excursion going to cost me?" I asked, looking in turn at both Englishmen. Frank had started cleaning his nails with a match. He looked pensively at Bill, who scratched his dark blond hair.

"I want you to know that my total capital consists of only a few pounds," I said, "and I just borrowed it from someone today. I am one of Castor's survivors who washed up here in Kano, and you know the saying, 'once burned, twice shy.'"

"We met Dan a few weeks ago," Bill said, a little annoyed, "and learned from him how Castor treated you fellows, so we are aware of that creep's methods. But take it from me, we'll treat you as fairly as we know how. Dan told us how you helped him through the various problems in the Sahara. That's why we trust you, Dutchy. You can square up with us when we arrive in Nairobi, or wherever we get stuck—whichever occurs first. But it won't be that expensive. We're only talking about petrol money, unless we have a breakdown."

I determined not to delay a decision any longer. I had to get out of Kano, and quickly. Whatever the outcome, these men were heading southeast, and that was the direction I wanted to go.

"When are we leaving?" I asked, stretching out my hand to seal the agreement.

"Great," Bill said. "Be here at seven in the morning, the day after tomorrow."

As we shook hands, the wick of the dying candle toppled over and the smelly room turned pitch black. The only visible gleam was the burning tip of Bill's cigarette.

A week later, at a snail's pace we neared the opposite bank of the Ubangi River. The native ferry on which we made the crossing consisted of ten dugout canoes held together by beams of rough lumber. Our army truck was precariously balanced atop these beams.

It was obvious that the fifteen oarsmen had been trained for their jobs. In unison they dipped their paddles into the silvery surface of the fast-flowing river. This rhythm was at the same time a kind of antiphony. An older African would chant a few words; the others would reply in chorus, and simultaneously lift and dip their paddles in perfect precision.

Viewed from the river, the bank and the low hills beyond it appeared to be a solid, deep-green jungle. Then, gradually, I could distinguish a myriad of vines and creepers spiraling toward the top of the trees. Lush, impenetrable, hostile country. This was the "green hell" of Africa.

In an aperture between enormous trees, I spotted two houses idyllically framed by purple bougainvillaeas, white frangipanis, and orange flamboyants. From a high flagpole near the first house hung the black, yellow, and red bands of the Belgian flag, representing the pride of the people of the Belgian Congo.

These houses apparently constituted the village of Zongo, marked in bold letters on the map. Though it was small, this village was of vital importance to us. Here resided the administrator of the area who would decide whether we could continue our journey through the Congo.

I glanced at my three relaxed English companions, sitting in the shade of the truck, watching the Africans wield their paddles. Clearly, they were enjoying the scenery, leaving any worrying to me. I was the interpreter, the one who dealt with various, often stubborn government officials.

A good relationship had built up between my three new companions and me, though not the intimate friendship I had enjoyed with Dan and Dick during the depressing desert days. With a mutual interest in reaching Nairobi, we four had divided the chores evenly and accomplished them without friction.

The oldest among us was Bill, a man in his early thirties. His whole being breathed authority, which was undoubtedly a result of service in the British army, where he had spent most of the war years. He wasted few words and generally made fast decisions. Reserved, always clean-shaven and well-groomed, he was a model product of the upper middle class. He had lost patience with postwar conditions in England and had decided on a new beginning in Kenya.

Frank was the opposite of Bill. Carefree and always happy, he seemed to be singing his way through life. As a mechanic, he was a valuable asset to our group and most of the time he did the driving as well. Bill and Frank had been friends for years and had even known each other in England. Frank also had set his eyes on Nairobi, where he hoped to begin his own business.

The last man in our party, Robert, was a tag-along like me. Bill and Frank had approached Robert in Kano, where he had been left behind by an overland group that had split after serious disagreements. Robert was the most indifferent and eccentric of the three Englishmen. He was content just to travel, and completing the journey didn't really matter to him. He appeared to be as broke as I was, but he counted on his British passport to open doors anywhere. His appearance didn't bother him, either, for he liked to dress in multicolored shirts and sometimes wore them inside out. That procedure saved frequent washings; he maintained that water was created only for drinking.

All in all, cooperation between us had been excellent. We accepted one another for what we were, and come what may, we determined to make this trip along the equator a reality.

We actually had not planned to cross the Ubangi here. There was supposed to be a ferry in considerably better shape than this several hundred miles up the river, but some French soldiers warned us that one of the larger bridges on the road to Bangassou was out and it would be impossible for us to pass. So, instead of going east, we had followed a road directly south.

We ended up crossing the river at Bangui, capital of French Equatorial Africa. After several hours of bargaining with the French colonial officials there, we were finally permitted to cross. It had taken about four hours to locate the leaky ferry. The first problem was how to get the truck aboard. All Frank's driving skills were needed for this maneuver. Would the whole string of lashed-together dugouts sink under the weight of the truck? Frank had edged the vehicle forward inch by inch, and the dugouts submerged and surfaced, rolled menacingly, righted, rolled again, and finally stabilized. With more faith than common sense, we had finally pushed the loaded ferry away from the shore.

Now here we were, pushing ashore on the Congo side of the river. Everyone's attention concentrated on the narrow strip of white, glistening sand ahead, and on the vine-draped houses in the background. Trees of all sizes competed for living space right down to the water's edge. Bromeliads with vivid red and yellow flowers abounded on the tree trunks and a choir of colorful birds provided sound effects.

With a soft thud, the string of dugouts came to a stop in the sand and we jumped to the gritty shore. After several tries, Frank managed to zig-zag the truck off the raft and through sand and mud to a higher elevation. As the truck stopped, I shouted, "We made it, men! We made it! Here we are, safely in the Congo!"

The question was, how safely? Coming down the path from the house with the Belgian flag was a man dressed in khaki shorts, shirt, and knee socks. He had to be the administrator of the area, the Belgian king's representative.

After the official niceties, which confirmed the man's position, I set about explaining the reason for our being here. He listened carefully, expressing only surprise, until he took a look at our passports. That was the end of good will.

"You have no permission to enter the Congo," he exclaimed coldly, shattering our hope of passing through the Congo without a hitch. He spread his legs across our path and put his hands on his hips as if to physically bar us from penetrating deeper into this part of the Belgian kingdom, the part entrusted to his care. Even the crew of almost naked Africans who had paddled us across looked puzzled, then stealthily made their way back to the cluster of dugouts.

As so many times before on my trip through the African continent, the nerve-wracking job of dealing with an unsympathetic official fell to me. Any colonial officer had the weight of the law behind him if he refused to let us enter his nation's territory. In our case, the circumstances could hardly have been worse. If we couldn't go forward, we couldn't go back either. The French officers on the other side of the river had made that clear.

Reload the truck on the dugouts and ride on down the river? To a landing point where there were no officials? One glance at the dugouts showed the impossibility of that thought: As the truck rolled off, the tied-together craft had broken into three splintered groups of dugouts. The boatmen were lashing it back together as best they could, but clearly it was badly weakened and would never hold up again under the weight of our truck.

The administrator maintained his stance squarely across our path. Looking past him, I saw that this path forked to the right beyond the first house and headed due south.

"As you can see, we desperately need help," I said and waited.

The administrator fixed his attention on the raft, and after staring at each of us in turn, made his decision. He would pass the problem to higher authority.

"This situation is impossible," he said. "I want all of you to report to my superior in Libenge, a hundred miles south of here. He will decide what to do with you."

He cleared his throat and added, "I see no other recourse."

I could have shouted for joy! That recourse suited us best of all.

The administrator stepped aside and we walked up the narrow, dark tunnel of a path to where the truck was parked. Quickly we got in and headed down the fork to the right, toward an uncertain future.

The dense underbrush was as impenetrable as a wall. Ferns and philodendrons fought for space on the tree trunks with other air plants and parasites. As our truck wormed its way deeper into the jungle, we were forever traveling in twilight. Only now and again a few slanting rays of the afternoon sun penetrated the heavy canopy of green. Multicolored butterflies by the millions darted in the shadows. The wheels of the truck left a double trail of crushed butterfly bodies.

In the endlessness of the Sahara, one could at least see approaching danger. Here, in the jungle, danger always loomed just ahead; even the humid air was laden with the anticipation of evil.

We crossed many little streams, each trying to find its way to the Ubangi somewhere to our right. Once in a while, a village made for a pleasant change in the scenery. A few huts, conical roofs covered with dried banana leaves, formed a circle in a cleared area. Now and then, I spotted African women walking along the path, but the moment the truck came into view, they hid under cover of the thicket. Only when we were a safe distance away would they reappear. Their clothing consisted of a small clump of beige-colored fiber in front and back. The men wore only loincloths. Some carried long spears and had a fierce look. Western civilization had not yet touched this part of Africa.

Slowly, the landscape changed. Patches of elephant grass filled gaps where the jungle had disappeared. Solitary palm trees lined the path here and there. At a fork in the road, Frank stopped and turned the motor off. Bill jumped out of the cab and suggested, "Let's take time out for a war council."

As we formed a circle around him, Bill said in a matter-of-fact tone, "You all realize we're in a country where we're not supposed to be. Circumstances forced us into a position we cannot change. The administrator of Zongo wanted us to report to his superior in the next village, but my instinct tells me not to awaken a sleeping dog.

"Why jeopardize what we have already gained?" he went on. "The next bureaucrat might not be so lenient. Let's take a chance and cross this country without papers. We've made it so far. We're loaded with petrol and by the time we need more I'm sure we'll run into some sucker with a soft spot for idiots. Food is no problem; we can keep swapping cigarettes and soap for bananas and eggs. Let's follow this left fork, which will take us due east.

"Since I come from the most democratic of nations," he concluded, "I have to give you a choice, so let's vote. Those who prefer to report officially to the Belgian authorities in

Libenge, don't move a limb. If you are willing to try your luck, raise your hand."

Four hands shot up toward the green leafy ceiling above us. Bill grinned and then laughed out loud.

"You're a darned good crew," he said. "Keep it up, laddies."

The moment we moved away from the Ubangi and turned toward the interior of the Congo, the scenery changed. On either side was a sea of light green grass, interrupted only by thousands of abandoned ant hills. Not a tree was in sight except for those on the horizon which marked the green belt of the jungle. Some of the rounded ant hill mounds were used by natives to built their homes on. These huts were constructed on stilts, apparently for a double precaution against flooding.

Perched on top of the truck, I realized how tall the grass was when I discovered a file of people making their way through it. Only their heads and the tips of their spears were visible. As they approached the path, wanting to cross, I could see that their bodies dripped with sweat.

Toward sunset Frank detected some irregularity in the hum of the engine and decided to check it out. But the tropical night was upon us in a matter of minutes. In the distance a native tam-tam sounded, and promptly another one responded from a different direction. A large blood-red moon rose slowly over the jungle's edge, illuminating the grassy plain with a spooky glow.

My assignment was to gather firewood, so I set out to collect some sticks to build a fire for the tea kettle. The Englishmen had impressed upon me that no matter where we were, tea was a must.

To my amazement, I was soon joined by four naked bodies carrying loads of wood, which they pitched on the fire. My precious kettle totally disappeared in the flames. The gleam in their eyes told me they were happy to show this foreigner how to light up an evening.

As the evening wore on, the light of the bonfire attracted hundreds of men and women, all standing around and gawking at us with curiosity. They kept a safe distance. None except the wood-carriers ventured close. Spreading our mosquito nets over some dry holes, we undressed under the watchful eyes of our observers and made ready for a night's rest.

The distant drone of tam-tams and the gurgling sounds of native voices were soon joined by the rocketing whistles of hungry, zooming mosquitoes. Somehow the mosquitoes found a way into our nets and the night was far from comfortable.

"I wonder what that fellow wants," Frank said more to himself than to me. "Look how he's acting. You think he's all right?"

I had already seen him from quite a distance. From his khaki shorts and light complexion, I concluded he must be European. But I agreed with Frank; judging by his erratic behavior, the man had a problem. Waving wildly with both arms, he did not move from the path, not even when we came very close. Frank put on the brakes and I jumped off to investigate.

"Monsieur, what is the matter?" I addressed him in French. "Can I do anything for you?"

"Please, stop a moment and have something to eat with me," he begged. "Please! All of you, I beg you. I am Pierre Dubon and all I want is for you to stay here for awhile."

I inquired further. "But why, Monsieur? Is there something you need?"

"Yes, please stay awhile," he said. "The reason is that I'm very lonely. Please tell your friends to pull over and I'll have an excellent meal prepared for you. If I can only talk to you for a few minutes."

Judging by his accent, Pierre Dubon had to be Belgian. But what was a good-looking young man doing in the Congo and what caused him to be so frantic? As I translated his wishes to Bill, Frank, and Robert, they were as puzzled as I, but they agreed to stay awhile to see what we could do for this desperate man.

The few days we had been in the Congo had passed without major problems. The jungle had changed into a type of savanna and the savanna again was overtaken by the primeval forest. I lost count of the streams and rivers we had crossed. Even the villages with the shy, naked men and women had become commonplace. For these people, greeting a passing white man seemed to be the most important event of the day. We had consistently minded our manners toward our African well-wishers, and we were not inclined to offer less courtesy to an agitated white man. Besides, the sight of him was a welcome change. So we ended up following the young Belgian to a double hut a distance off the road.

As we approached, two locals in ragged short pants appeared and received instructions from the Belgian by way of a series of sharp sounds—an order in their dialect to prepare a meal.

As I entered the first hut, my eyes took quick inventory: two old chairs, four empty cases, a small table, and a homemade kitchen cabinet. That was the furniture. A bed with mosquito netting draped over it stood in the adjoining hut. This double shack suggested double misery and wasn't exactly a bachelor's dream.

The moment we sat down, Pierre Dubon bombarded me with questions. "Where are you from? What are you doing here? Where are you going?" I had hardly begun answering the first question when he was ready with two more.

Soon it appeared that this young man wasn't really interested in our history or future plans. All he wanted was to communicate with someone, to let go of the pent-up emotions and feelings he had not been able to share with another white person for quite some time. Except for a little nervousness and bags under his eyes, he looked perfectly healthy. Clean-shaven and dressed in a good-fitting khaki outfit, he certainly did not give the impression of being a social outcast.

It required little prompting to find out who and what he was. Pierre was graduated from a university in Belgium with a medical degree. Soon thereafter he had signed with the government to fulfill a three-year contract in the tropics. His assignment was this out-of-the-way corner in the Congo where he was to be a modern medicine man for the surrounding tribes.

"But, sir, believe me," he said, "this kind of life is hard to take. Europeans don't have the faintest idea how large this country really is. The district I'm supposed to keep disease-free is larger than all of Belgium. In all of this area there are only five Europeans, and they live hundreds of miles from each other.

"Sure," he continued, "being idealistic and a student in medicine, one has high expectations of the Congo. I had expected to live in a beautiful, exotic land, to serve these unspoiled natives, and to conquer this vast, virgin forest. But just live here for a few years in the reality of it all—without change, without entertainment, without friends or family, hardly ever able to talk to your equals—and you'll soon change your opinion about the life in this green Utopia.

"This exotic land is not appealing when one has to put up with clouds of blood-thirsty mosquitoes, the unbearable heat, and the dreadful jungle, where even the color green becomes so intolerable that it hurts one's eyes.

"Then these unspoiled natives! They are the most primitive tribes of the Congo, but no one ever told me how primitive they are in their stupidity. And unspoiled? What a farce! Murder, adultery, sorcery, rape are daily occurrences with these innocent, charming natives who are supposed to be living in paradise."

With a deep sigh, Pierre continued, "Oh, it sounds so nice on paper or in a discussion in the classroom: 'the unsurpassed splendor of these large virgin forests.' You will quickly change your mind about the beauty of it all when the brush tears up your clothes and your skin and the tropical diseases play havoc with your health. Especially when you have lost your way in this 'exotic jungle-land.'"

The young doctor rattled on. Feelings of disappointment, loneliness, and perhaps some resentment were now put into words, possibly for the first time in months. He made it abundantly plain that he could not cope with the wilderness around him. But who could blame Pierre for that? The hard realities he had encountered had not lined up with the dreams and ideals of a youthful student.

"What are your duties?" I inquired, partly out of genuine interest and partly because I felt it did the doctor more good to talk than to listen.

"To keep the local diseases under control—diseases such as malaria, cholera, venereal diseases, yellow fever, elephantiasis, and sleeping sickness, just to name a few. All in all, it is a never-ending stream of misery."

"Aren't you married?" I tried to keep him talking.

"What would a white woman do in this dreadful hole?" he responded. "Die from some kind of illness? Slowly pine away of homesickness? No, there is no room for white women in this climate. Higher on the plateaus, maybe, but not here. The land around here is too low and too dangerous for your health."

"You said you were waiting for us on the path long before we showed up," I continued. "How did you know we were on the way?"

"Simple," he said. "For quite some time I had heard the tam-tams beating back and forth. When that happens you know the people are passing information, so I asked my servant what was going on and he informed me that some white men were on their way in a large truck. So I waited on the trail to make sure I wouldn't miss you."

Two black men entered shyly and a little awkwardly, bearing a couple of steaming pans which they set before us.

"What a fantastic treat!" We four travelers seemed to echo this sentiment together.

"That looks a lot better than bananas for breakfast, lunch, and supper," Robert added.

Indeed, it was. We evenly divided among us the fried chicken, baked potatoes, and pineapple. Pierre Dubon refused everything; he was hungry only for conversation, not food, he said.

"Tell me, why are you following this path?" he asked. "Hardly ever does a European pass by here. They usually take the ferry at Bangassou."

"Well, we couldn't," I said. "One of the bridges apparently had caved in along the road, so there was no alternative but to come this way." I carefully avoided mention of the administrator at Zongo.

He nodded, apparently satisfied with my explanation. Lunch was over now, and our empty plates showed only well-cleaned chicken bones. Still, our host didn't want us to leave.

He tried to persuade us to linger longer, but we were restless and intent on putting as much distance as possible between us and the administrator.

Shaking hands with the lonely doctor, we thanked him for his hospitality. He shrugged his shoulders and said softly, "Non, messieurs, I am the one who really ought to thank you. Believe me, I feel much better already now that I have been able to air my grievances. I'm grateful you were willing to stop and hear me out. You'll never know how much you have helped me."

The truck picked up speed, and glancing back once more, I focused for the last time on the sagging figure of the lonely young man standing in the road, watching us fade from sight.

"Look at that!" Frank shouted. "Do you see what I see, or am I dreaming? Could those be petrol drums?" He pointed to five steel drums standing under two huge mango trees.

"No, you're not dreaming," I said. "They surely could be fuel tanks."

He pulled the truck over beside the drums and stopped. We jumped out to inspect them. We were still on the same trail we had started on, though now it led in a southeasterly direction. According to our map, we had reached Yakoma, a village that looked more attractive than the others we had seen.

Our travel had had its worrisome moments, but no major mishap. Our diet of bananas was monotonous. We had eaten red bananas, square bananas, green bananas, wild ones, cultivated ones, and even some the size of a finger. Our nights had been spent around campfires surrounded by naked onlookers, mysterious sounds in the jungles, and the buzzing of thousands of insects.

Recently, though, a real problem threatened: We had not come across any gasoline and our supply was perilously low. That we should come upon five drums of it now was little short of providential.

We noticed a house with a European appearance, set back from the road and all but hidden in the trees. As we stood looking, three white men emerged from the front door, calling to us,

"Bonjour! Bonjour, messieurs! I bet you are ready for a beer. Come in and make yourselves comfortable."

All three men were short, with straight black hair and olive complexion. As they introduced themselves, it became clear by their names, Trindade, Maceio, and Silva, that they were Portuguese. They were well dressed in khaki shorts and colored shirts and seemed genuinely pleased to see us. We followed them into the front room, which turned out to be a store. Racks with brightly colored cloths reached the ceiling. African cooking utensils were stacked on the floor. Small packages of food rations, soap, and tools made up the bulk of the merchandise. Anything the local people might desire was available.

We passed through the store into a comfortable sitting room. Before going farther, we asked about gas for the truck.

"Ah, no problem whatsoever," Silva said. He was apparently the leader of the three. "You've seen those drums outside? They are full. We always keep plenty on hand. Feel free to fill up."

"I'm afraid there might be a problem," I said. "To be honest, we have no Belgian or French francs. All we have is English money. The question is, can you accept pounds sterling?"

In Portuguese the three talked the problem over, then Silva smiled and said, "Gentlemen, an acquaintance in Nigeria will know how to exchange them. Now go and take what you need."

Before our benefactors could change their minds, Bill, Frank, and Robert went to work filling the truck tank and every can and jug we had.

Meanwhile, our hosts had set about providing refreshments. As they scurried around gathering bottles of cold beer and glasses, I put my feet on an ottoman, leaned back, and marveled at the unexpected blessings that life so often delivers.

"You believe in the good life, I see." I spoke in English to lead to a conversation we all could join in.

"I believe we deserve a little comfort," Silva picked up on the English, "considering that we are spending the greater part of our lives in the heart of Africa. We make our living in the native store. We voluntarily abandoned the old civilization back

137

home to operate this trading post in the middle of nowhere. When we have made enough to live on comfortably in Portugal, we will retire and sell our part of the store to someone else, and live out our lives back home."

By now, Bill, Frank, and Robert had come back to join us. Their beer was waiting for them. Bill filled a glass: "To one day at a time," he said, "and especially to nice days like this."

"That goes for all of us," I said.

"Especially for me," Frank chimed in. "I'm the one who looks after the truck, who tries to keep us on the road. Frankly, this morning, I wouldn't have given a shilling for our chances of finding fuel. Suddenly, thanks to you, there is no more cause for fear."

Our attention turned from Frank as yet another person joined the party, another European, a north European from all appearances.

"I am Jan de Lange," he announced himself. "I saw your truck parked in front of the store and curiosity drew me in. Just had to know who was traveling through Yakoma."

A Dutchman! One who spoke unaccented British English and even bore himself with the suggestion of British dignity. The Portuguese had spoken earlier of someday selling their part of the store. Could this be the owner of the other part?

At that moment, there was a rumble of thunder and a glance outside showed dark clouds gathering. We were in for a tropical cloudburst.

"I say," Jan de Lange began, "why not have supper with me and then spend the night here?" He started by addressing me and then turned to face the others. "I've got a decent place and with a storm coming there's no use going on. You'll just get stuck on the trail or maybe have to wait it out on a river bank. And when one of these streams is swollen by a sudden rainstorm, no native will ferry you across. Take your pick, but I think you all will be more comfortable here."

He looked at me again. "What do you say?"

We voted unanimously to wait out the storm.

Jan's Dutch nationality having been established, my three friends elected to stay with the Portuguese so I could enjoy a relaxed evening with a compatriot.

As I walked with Jan to the other side of the village, I learned that in fact he did own part of the store. He had other businesses, too. When we reached the place where he lived, I was surprised to see not only his house through the trees, but also a number of other buildings.

"Is all this yours, Jan?" I asked. I had already learned that he was single and thus not in need of expansive dwelling.

"No," he answered. "All this belongs to the company I work for. Those buildings are just warehouses and garages."

I was puzzled. "What possible interest could any company have in this area? I haven't seen any evidence of anything saleable—except lumber."

Once free of the others, we reverted to Dutch and in our own language we grew talkative. "Come along and I'll show you," Jan said with pride in his voice. He led the way to one of the warehouses.

"Ever heard of the culture system?" he asked. "It means the native people must relinquish one-fifth of their crops to the government in lieu of paying taxes in money. Now, in some cases, the colonial government does not levy the taxes itself but sells the right to collect them to certain companies. Of course, these companies buy this right because they can make a profit from it. I am, in reality, an appointed tax collector for a European company.

"Here, however, there are difficulties since the locals don't produce much except a little cotton in some small clearings. That's usually as far as their interest in agriculture goes. By right, I receive one-fifth of their crop as tax money and then buy up the other four-fifths."

Concluding his job description, Jan reached for the doorknob of the first warehouse. A musty smell assailed my nostrils the moment the door was opened. The last light of day streaked through a closed window in the opposite wall.

"See," Jan said, "this is what the natives get in exchange for the part of their crop that I buy." He pointed to piles of old, wrinkled American army uniforms. Olive-green coats, pants, and caps by the thousands lay on the shelves. The uniforms in which American youths had fought and won battles around the world had come to this miserable, moldering end.

Jan explained how the procedure worked. "My company bought up these masses of old army clothes in the USA and shipped the stuff here for disposal. As the natives bring in their cotton, I pay for it with these piles of junk."

I stood for a moment in disbelief, followed quickly by disgust.

"To me, this 'culture system,' as you call it, sounds more like exploitation than honest pursuit of gain. Is this the light of civilization that is supposed to bring the natives out of the Dark Ages?"

I stared again, in total loathing, at the shelf loads of rotting fabric.

In reaction to my outburst, Jan de Lange explained placatingly, "The natives don't have to accept this stuff; they usually choose a variety of knick-knacks instead. Or they can make direct payment of their taxes in money. I try to comply with their wishes. But in general," he added slowly, "their crops are paid for with these." He ran his index finger along a row of fatigues.

Leaving that first warehouse, I scrutinized the young Dutchman from the side. He was nearer twenty-seven than thirty. His square chin announced firmness and his penetrating eyes took in every detail. It was hard to believe he would let the Africans decide for themselves the manner of payment for their work. His company had hired the right man for their purposes. Jan de Lange was more than equal to the back country of the Congo. Here was a taskmaster not hobbled by ethics or compassion.

"What do you do in your spare time?" I asked. "Don't you get bored?"

"Bored?" he grinned. "No, there's no time for idleness. Nearly every day I go out to visit one tribe or another. This time of the year is cotton harvest and I have to see that it comes in on time and gets stored safely away in my barns. Then I have to go around persuading the natives to plant again—cotton or whatever other crop can make a profit. If there is time left, which is seldom, I go canoeing. I have made myself a real canoe and I go paddling up and down the Uele River over there. Then, again, I am often occupied with my private enterprise."

He stopped, leaving the subject dangling.

We had come to Jan's house, which had a commanding view over the jungle. In the distance I could see, shimmering among the trees, the majestic river where this Dutchman went canoeing. Entering the front door, Jan strode directly to a room in the rear.

"Come," he motioned to me. "My 'private enterprise.'"

He looked with satisfaction over the room before us. Along the walls were literally hundreds of native spears, quite a few in copper and all different in style and length. On the floor I counted more than a dozen interesting-looking drums in many sizes. The rest of the room was filled with still other native curios: carved heads, musical instruments, bows and arrows, pottery, and other objects I couldn't even identify.

Looking more closely at this vast array of native-made wares, the realization struck me that all were brand new and seemingly unused.

"My, you have some kind of collection here!" I was genuinely overwhelmed, realizing the potential sales value of the objects in front of me.

"Not bad, eh? Not bad at all," the Dutchman's eyes swept over the lot. "You like my curio collection?"

"I sure do," I said, "but surely, they're not just for your own private collection?"

"Are you kidding?" he laughed. "What would I do with this stuff? Didn't I tell you this is my 'private enterprise'? My own private business? When I came here I soon realized that every native *always* makes the same kind of spear, the same kind of drum, the same kind of everything. They probably have done so from time immemorial. These people have not had a new idea in centuries, so I hit on a plan—a bright one. I took some pieces of iron or copper with me and told the spear makers, 'Here is some material. Try to come up with something new, something different, original. I'm not interested in ancient crafts. If you make the blade a little wider, shorten the shaft a little, add some fancy points here and there, then we'll have a new model. Never mind how well it throws; I don't care about that. I do care about how it looks. It's got to be different from anything your forefathers made.'"

Jan waved his hand toward the collection. "Here is the result," he said proudly. "You realize that all these items are modified, but they are still made by the same tribe and similar objects were often made by the same man."

"How do you sell them?" I asked.

"I send these 'art objects' to museums all over the world," he said. "The curators are more than pleased to receive such extraordinary examples of 'original' African artifacts. The more variety the better."

I had no doubt that this scheming Dutchman was doing a roaring business. But I found his methods utterly appalling.

"You know," he went on, "art critics like to be fooled; and the common man—a man like me—has to make use of that if he wants to get ahead."

He sounded as if he were defending himself against my unspoken thoughts. Or was he just waiting for approval?

"You say you apply the same methods with these drums, the bows and arrows, and all the rest?" I asked, keeping my voice neutral.

"Oh, yes," he replied, "especially these drums. The natives only made one or two sizes in the past. But, thanks to my instructions, they now make them in a wide range of sizes, from this puny one . . ." he picked up one only four or five inches wide ". . . to that behemoth over there that's more than three feet wide." The drum he pointed to was magnificent, taller than it was wide, surrounded by animal fur.

"Why, today," he said, "I can deliver a complete Congo drum orchestra." He started beating the hides on the three nearest tam-tams, imitating the droning drumbeat we had heard so often along the trail during the past week.

I had to admit, this young scoundrel had no lack of imagination, or, for that matter, of adaptability. He had learned not only how to accept his environment but how to exploit it to the fullest. What a contrast to the Belgian doctor we had met a few days ago, who had not come to grips with the challenges of his daily life and was sinking steadily deeper into despair. The contrast was startling. This Dutchman, far from feeling lonely and depressed, was positively euphoric. From the way he went about his "business," he found life one big joke. He enjoyed himself immensely, in spite of the inevitable day-to-day hardships of being in one of the remotest, most primitive corners of the entire world.

"These natives are not bad at all," Jan said as we sat down to dinner. "You just have to know how to manipulate them. In Africa, there are two principles you have to apply in order to survive: First, it's a matter of keeping these people in their place; and secondly, of mastering their language as quickly as you can."

That he had managed to master both parts of this principle was abundantly clear in the effortless way he ordered the servants around in their own dialect. No African chief could have surpassed him.

That night, as I tossed about under a heavy mosquito net, there was an ear-splitting blast, and then another, and with that the storm broke. Tons of water poured down. Would the trail now be impassable? And for how long? There was no possibility of sleep as I lay listening to the roaring downpour soak the earth.

By morning, though, the rain had subsided, leaving the world very clean and flesh. Looking out from the house, it was evident that the Uele River in the valley below could not be crossed. Wild and enormously swollen, the murky flood rushed past.

"Just wait a few hours," Jan counseled, "and you'll be amazed at how fast the water level drops. The real rains haven't started yet. These cloudbursts are only indications that the rainy season is on its way."

I could only hope he was right. The trail was the one highway in this region and it lay near the riverbank. Getting stuck in waterlogged mud could stall us for days.

After a breakfast of real bread, butter, and slices of canned ham, we stepped outside to begin the walk back to the Portuguese store, where I could rejoin my partners. As we started down the steps, a young, well-proportioned native girl of about fourteen, wearing a pretty cotton dress, emerged from the woods in front and began smiling and swinging her hips. The flowery dress was quite a change from the common grass skirts or pieces of old cloth draped about the hips of most of the local women.

"Well," I said admiringly, "isn't she pretty?"

Jan only scowled and immediately began shouting and gesturing. The girl appeared not to notice. She seemed impervious to whatever he was saying. At last he took a few running steps toward her, still shouting and waving for her to go away. At that, the girl turned her back and slowly sauntered off.

"What does she want, Jan?" I asked.

"Me," he answered irritably. He looked around at me. "I mean it," he said. "I can't get rid of her. She wants to become my woman, as they say here. This coming practically up to the house—it's the latest phase. It started three days ago. Who knows what comes next? These people know I'm not married and they've decided that I need a woman, any woman. That's one of the curses of the Congo. Just about every unattached European male who comes here ends up living with a native woman—not that these girls have to be pressured into the situation. For them, life with a white man will be much better than they've been used to all their lives.

"Take our Portuguese friends," he concluded. "Every one of them lives with a native girl. I am the only European for miles around who has not taken up the practice yet." He walked on silently.

Were Jan's moral standards higher than his business ethics? Or did he simply look down on all the native people, girls included? I leaned in favor of the latter explanation.

"Well, Jan," I said, "at some point she's bound to give up."

"And then there'll be another one pestering around," he grumbled. "I just hope I don't find myself having to face down the whole Ngobandi tribe one of these days."

In the next few hours, the weather cleared up considerably and the swollen river subsided. This foretaste of the weather to come enhanced our resolve to move on quickly. We had to escape from this jungle while we still could. We cut our good-byes short and set out once more on the now treacherous, slippery trail to the unknowns ahead. But there was one heartening thought: The farther we advanced into the heart of Africa, the less chance, we thought, of being apprehended. The Congo police, if indeed they existed at all, would surely not come looking for us this deep in the territory. Surely they must have their hands full with other problems.

Inky darkness enveloped us. Only by the flashes of lightning could we see our surroundings. Even Frank and Robert had ceased their banter and sat glumly staring ahead. More strokes of lightning; more crashes of thunder! The jungle animals that usually produced a cacophony of sound after sunset were hushed, as if waiting in suspense for some tremendous finale. Warm drops of rain began penetrating the thick tree tops.

We had stopped for the night, getting ready for another downpour. According to Bill's map, we couldn't be too far from the village of Mambasa in the Ituri Forest of the eastern Congo. However, the consensus was to wait out the storm on the spot. We knew that when the rains came, they would come with such force that water would soon surround us like a wet glass wall. We could expect the truck to slide off the trail into the brush. And we would have to keep alert for giant tree trunks that might be split by the lightning.

As we hunched together waiting for the worst, the lightning began to diminish. Then the rain. And when the myriad of crickets recovered their voices and began shrilling into the night, we understood that the storm had ended.

Any attempt to move the truck, however, would be disastrous until the surface of the trail at least partially dried out. That would not be soon. So we set out on foot to find a small village, shown on the map to be only four or five kilometers ahead. It turned out to be closer than that—less than an hour's walk. As soon as we reached it, I was sent scouting for an empty native hut, or preferably, a special hut for travelers, called *gite d'etappe*, which could usually be found throughout the Congo. It wouldn't do at all to be caught outside if the storm should happen to return.

But indoor accommodations were not to be found. Apologetically, the natives got the message across that there was no gite d'etappe here. So our choice was to make our way back to the truck, which would at least provide cover for us, or stay here in the village, outside, but around a campfire. The campfire would not protect us from a storm, but it would be of some use in warding off the mosquitoes. Tramping back to the truck over the slippery mud seemed like too much trouble. We decided to take our chances where we were.

The moment the locals saw that these four Europeans were about to honor their village with an overnight stay, they went into hurried consultation and then scattered to organize the obligatory entertainment for their guests. They kindled small fires in front of their huts and fed them with heaps of wood until the huge, dancing flames of a dozen fires lit the dense vegetation around the village.

Someone struck a few blows on an ancient drum. For a fraction of a minute complete silence reigned over the jungle. It was broken by the drumming again, more insistent this time and for a longer period. In front of the hut closest to us someone responded by hammering with all his might on a drum more than two feet in diameter. This was apparently the signal to all within earshot that a party was about to begin and to "come as you are."

Scantily clothed men and women swarmed in from all directions to gather in the open space in front of the huts. The tam-tams seemed to compete for loudness. The three drummers alternated in style, first furiously beating the vibrating hides with their hands, then with sticks. Pandemonium broke out as shouting people leaped forward into the open space, slamming their feet into the reddish soil, their bodies writhing to the ever-quickening rhythm of the drums. Faster and faster the throb of the tam-tams, faster and faster the leaps and twists of the prancing natives. Some of the men had put on old, white shirts; and in the flaring light of the flames, those shirts cast a ghostlike aura over the increasing hysteria of the scene. Muscular arms groped for the heavens, and wild, rolling eyes cruised unseeingly as bodies jostled and contorted in other-worldly torment.

Fascinated, we looked on, but with sobering fear over how this performance might conclude. It seemed to be intensifying. Mewing and shouting had risen to a hellish pitch, a bombardment of noise unrelated to either the rhythm or pitch of the drum rolls. Not a sound from the jungle could penetrate this cacophony.

But were we listening, yet not hearing . . . ?

Abruptly, the dancers stopped, poised in whatever position they were in when the drumming stopped. The silence was stark, a total cutoff of all noise and movement.

Ears strained to pick up a sound.

Then I heard it—a faint cry emanating from one of the nearby huts, and suddenly I understood. Somehow, through the ear-splitting noise of drums and pounding feet and shouts and screams, everyone—except the four of us—had heard that beautiful sound, the barely audible whimper of a newborn baby. With laughter in their eyes, the panting Africans looked at us, repeatedly pointing toward the hut where the faint crying persisted.

In deepest respect, they quietly disassembled.

The night once more belonged to the jungle.

The first rays of the sun streaked past giant trees around the village where a couple of natives tried to get my attention. One, a short, stocky man who called himself Pilo and even spoke a little comprehensible French, pointed to a hut and repeated, "Monsieur! Look! Look!"

The young woman I saw there was the one who had given birth just a few hours ago. Now, glowing with happiness, she wanted to show off her infant son to the alien visitors. We patted the baby and cooed over his tiny form in what we hoped were internationally understood sounds of admiration.

Standing by, Pilo repeatedly informed us, in case we still did not grasp the facts, "See? Is boy! Born last night."

At various points along the way the truck engine had given us problems, and because it was another thousand miles to Nairobi, Bill and Frank suggested we make whatever repairs we could. This would be better than risking a serious breakdown later. My own concerns focused more on the risks of delay, considering the likelihood of unabating rainstorms. I was not, however, in a position to impose my point of view on the others. So they started to work on the motor. Countless women, children, and a few scattered men formed a tight circle around the Englishmen as they began to remove and examine various parts.

Considering what to do with myself while they worked, I realized that, for all the traveling I'd done, I had not had a chance to delve into native customs anywhere. Catching the eye of Pilo, who was standing idly with the others near the truck, I beckoned him over. I managed to explain to him that I wanted to know about the ways of life in the area.

A man only four feet tall, with yellowish-brown skin suddenly emerged from the forest. He had a bow slung over his shoulder and, by a strap dangling from his forehead, he held a carcass of meat. Another strap around his waist was tied to a woven quiver with a few arrows sticking out. He made straight for the chief's hut.

"Who's that, Pilo?" I asked. "That little fellow over there?"

"Pygmy," came the answer.

"They're not members of your tribe, are they?" I asked.

Pilo snorted his ridicule. "No. Never! Cannot be."

"Do they live with your tribe?" I continued to dig for information.

"No." Pilo's one- and two-word answers were improving my knowledge of local relationships only a short step at a time.

"Where do they live?"

"In forest," Pilo waved to the wall of trees from which the Pygmy had emerged.

"Why did this Pygmy come to your village?"

"Come trade." Pilo gave me a searching look, and anticipating the next questions, added, "Come trade meat for iron."

"Why does the Pygmy want iron?"

"Need iron for arrows. Need arrows to kill meat."

I was finally able to glean the information that the tribes of this area, the Lese and Lenda, had carried on this same trade with the Pygmies for centuries—iron for meat and skins.

The Pygmies were the professional hunters for the lot of them, an arrangement that enabled the tribes to settle down more or less and the Pygmies to migrate with the game, which they preferred to do so long as the movement was within the perimeters of the forest. The Pygmies outstripped everybody else in agility and hunting skill within the overgrown jungles, and thus there was no incentive for the pattern to change.

"Tell me, Pilo," I began again, "do they live far from here?"

"Not far," he answered. Then, clearly bored with my questions, he had an inspiration of how to stop them. Rising to his feet, he motioned me to follow. "Come," he said, "you come see Pygmy place. Come."

I looked to see how the truck repairs were coming. "How long will this take?" I called. Bill's grumpy voice called back, "Who knows? Three, four hours, if we're lucky." He talked a little longer, naming the truck's disorders, but I was already on my way, following Pilo toward the forest.

For the first quarter hour the path was not bad, almost level as it twisted among colossal trees. The heat was appalling. Not a breath of air penetrated the tree tops, which formed a single, giant umbrella over us. My clothes were almost instantly soaked with perspiration, an object lesson in the practicality of a loincloth.

Trees of various sizes had fallen across the path, pulling down with them a network of vines. We often had to clamber over and through a maze of decaying timber. Resilient branches scourged my face and giant thorns tore my clothes. Twisted vines thicker than a man's arm wound up to the tree tops where sunlight was faintly visible. I tripped and fell and tripped again. Somehow the path had disappeared. There was no more trail, no visible indication of where we were going. I instinctively followed Pilo, who in this jumble of brush, trees, and creepers seemed to have no trouble finding his way. Hundreds of birds overhead shrieked and screeched. The squeals of monkeys high on the branches sounded diabolical.

Nearly suffocated by the sweltering heat, I sat on a huge fallen tree. As we rested quietly, the tiny figure of a man scurried by. At amazing speed and without a word, the Pygmy slid over the tree trunks and between the mess of branches. He didn't even glance at us. He had his left arm stuck through a small bow and on his hip hung a matted, woven quiver.

"He warn others we come," Pilo said, matter-of-factly.

He was correct. Ten minutes later a shrill howling sounded ahead of us. The Pygmy had arrived home and was reporting the news.

When we had slithered and scampered for more than an hour, Pilo finally announced, pointing to a clearing on his left, "We here." A small area had been cleared of shrubs and underbrush. Only the tall trees had not been touched.

From one of the huts, a four-foot-tall Pygmy came to meet us. His face was wrinkled and weather-beaten. On his protruding jawbones and cheeks, he had smeared black powder. Observing his total physique, I noticed that some parts of his body seemed out of proportion. He had a large head, heavy body, long arms, and short legs. His nose was wide at the nostrils, contrasting strangely with his thin lips.

"Pygmy chief," Pilo said. Shyly, the old man stepped closer, evaluating the white man in front of him. I let Pilo do all the conversing while I set out to examine more closely this unique clearing and its inhabitants. It was clear that this spot was only a temporary homestead, and very temporary at that. Because the Pygmies lived almost entirely off hunting, it never took long for them to wipe out the game in their immediate surroundings. Then they would follow the game and settle again for another few short weeks.

What intrigued me most was their small huts. They bent a dozen supple branches and stuck both ends in the ground to form a dome frame. They covered this frame with leaves, giving the Pygmy his home, which usually would not be higher than four feet, six inches. The entrance was narrow and low to the ground, probably to keep the rains out. They had to crawl on all fours to get in or out.

Because they lived with frequent heavy rains and had no medical assistance, their lives were constantly threatened by disaster and disease. But in spite of these impositions, the tiny forest dwellers had survived for centuries. With great skill they set up their camouflaged traps and with unsurpassed finesse they shot the okapi and antelope in the densest of vegetation. They would even stalk an elephant, hit him with poisoned arrows, then track him down relentlessly until he dropped dead.

There were few Pygmy men and women in the village. We saw mostly children.

"Are there no more people than these living here?" I asked as Pilo came to join me.

"During day, Pygmy men hunt like white men would. During day Pygmy women seek herbs, like white women cook. But night time comes, all Pygmies around fire."

It was clear that we had come exploring at the wrong time. Everyone was on the job.

The disorderly camp was far from attractive. It was filthier than any other village I had seen in central Africa. A little disillusioned and sad about the plight of the Pygmies, I started my trip back through the dreadful forest with Pilo. Under my arm, I held tightly to a flat quiver made out of reed, which contained half a dozen poisoned arrows, a gift from the little old chief.

Back at Pilo's village, Bill, Frank, and Robert had miraculously completed the repairs on the truck, and were anxiously awaiting my return. A tumultuous farewell followed, as the entire population of the village flocked to the road. Pilo stood in the front, repeating his promise to me, "Monsieur, you come back, you see more Pygmies."

Not many hours of the day remained, but Bill insisted we try to cover at least a few more miles. We couldn't go fast, because the path was narrow and steep again. At certain sections the trail was nearly closed in by gargantuan trees and evergreen foliage. Huge branches hosted a great variety of air plants.

Toward sunset, angry clouds drifted in again and rolling thunder announced another violent storm.

"There's a campfire, just off the road," Bill announced. "We'll have to look for shelter. Maybe this village has a hut where we can stay for the night."

As we came closer, the campfire turned out to be light from a solitary house—possibly the home of a European family.

"Maybe these people can put us up," Frank suggested. "The place is big enough."

The rain was already pouring down and we all made a dash for the house's large porch. I knocked impatiently, and soon a middle-aged white man opened the door. His only prominent feature was a sharp nose. His graying hair was well groomed. He stood stooped, waiting for us to say something.

"Monsieur would have a room where we could spend the night?" I asked in French. "We've been caught off guard in this storm."

The man shrugged and said nothing. He could have been deaf for all I could tell. I repeated the question louder, but he only threw up his hands and shrugged once more.

"I don't think he understands, Dutchy," said Robert, standing behind me.

"If y'all speak English," the man said, "why don't you try that on me?" He had the obvious twang of one from the American South.

"Well, sir," I said, "we were caught by this rain and wondered if you could put us up for the night?"

He let his eyes wander over each of us. "Can any of you play chess?" he asked, beginning to smile.

Was this to be a trade-off, I wondered—a game of chess in exchange for shelter for the night?

"I play chess," I said.

"In that case, come right in." He led us into the living room. The place was clean, well-kept, and homey. Family pictures hung on the wall, and around the room were various mementos.

A clock ticked on the wall. Four chairs of bamboo were arranged around a table, and in a corner stood a wheelchair.

"My wife is in the States," the man said, "but make yourselves at home. On the porch there's room enough for y'all to sleep."

Without wasting another moment, he went directly to the closet and came back with a chess set. A minute later he had the pieces lined up for battle.

"We may as well start right away," he said, looking expectantly at me.

"We'll prepare something to eat," Bill said, leaving the room with his friends.

"I'll help," I offered. I was tired and not at all enthusiastic about getting involved in a complex battle of chess.

"Just play the man, Dutchy," Robert said, obviously wanting to make sure we would have shelter for the night.

Before I sat down, the American moved his queen's pawn and looked up at me as if to say, "Move!"

I wondered what was going on in his mind. What made him attack me so decidedly in this game? Couldn't he communicate? He had hardly spoken a dozen words since we entered his home, and come to think of it, I didn't even know his name. What was he leading up to?

Not willing to face humiliating defeat, I played my best and the American gallantly defended his positions. Conversation was taboo and the only sound my competitor allowed to escape from his lips was an occasional deep sigh.

Our game lasted about two hours. My English friends had finished supper, and not hearing them stirring on the porch, I concluded that they must have gone to sleep, enjoying a well-deserved rest. However, the moment our first game was finished, the old man lined up his pawns for the next contest. Since I had skipped dinner and was totally exhausted, I wasn't in the mood for another battle of the mind. But since I didn't want to disappoint this solitary man, I gave in and was soon locked in another match.

It was doubtful that this American would encounter many partners in the Ituri Forest. Halfway through the game he suggested, "Can't you stay here? I mean, can't you locate here? I wish you lived close by."

Those were the only words he had uttered in six hours.

By midnight, I was bushed. I told my opponent that I was more than ready for the night. Passing his fingers through his graying hair, my chess-hungry host insisted, "Only on condition that you'll continue this game tomorrow morning."

Seeing no other way out, I gave in.

"Come along," he ordered, getting up. I followed his bent figure outside. The rain had stopped, but leaves and branches overhead dripped intermittently at the slightest breeze.

Hidden among the trees was a small building. The American pushed the door open and struck a match. In the dim light I saw a few beds. Toward the back of the room there was a kind of divider.

"You can sleep here," he said, and turning on his heels left me in total darkness.

Feeling my way to the first bed and finding it empty, I practically fell on it fully clothed. All night, I dreamt of playing chess with giant pieces on a huge board.

"Were you able to find out anything about our host?" Robert asked the moment I joined my friends for breakfast of tea and bananas.

"You should have, Dutchy," Frank joined in. "You rated higher than we did. You got to sleep in a real bed."

"I don't know any more than you do," I said. "The man doesn't talk, he just sighs and plays chess. The place I slept looked like a dispensary or clinic. He must be a doctor, or a missionary—maybe both."

A sorry-looking group of Africans had gathered in front of the small building where I had slept. It was obvious they had come for help. One man limped toward the door, his leg wrapped in a filthy blood-stained rag. Close to the building, he plopped down on the wet ground. A boy appeared with a badly swollen arm. A worried mother rocked a crying, hollow-eyed baby.

The taciturn American appeared at the front door. We were about ready to leave, but the moment the old man laid eyes on me, he half ordered, "Remember your promise to first finish last night's game."

Objections were of no use. I had to complete the game. In the living room, the pieces on the chessboard stood silent, waiting to be engaged in battle once again.

As I finally laid down my king in defeat, the graying man got up, took a white coat from the closet and put it on.

"Are you a doctor?" I asked.

"Yes, and a missionary. My wife used to be with me. So was my only son. But my boy is a paraplegic. He had to go back to the States and my wife had to go with him."

Speaking softly, in short sentences, he cast a sad glance at the empty wheelchair under the family pictures. Standing pensively, he looked older, probably from grief and loneliness. He waited a few moments and then said, "If you pass by here again, come and play chess with me."

Without another word, he disappeared toward the clinic.

At the Congo's border with Uganda, the Belgian government official was at first uncooperative, showing no intention of letting us through. In keeping with British dignity, a trait I had somehow taken on, none of us panicked but simply determined to wait for another day and another opportunity. Strange as it seemed, the officer had a change of heart overnight. The next morning, unexpectedly, he even seemed eager to please us. There were no further questions, and without any hindrance we were allowed into British Uganda Protectorate.

Crossing the highlands of Uganda and Kenya was the smoothest part of our trip along the equator. Once we arrived in Nairobi, it meant another time of farewell. The truck had reached its destination and was handed over to the owner. Out of money, my three English pals went to look for work. Our paths separated for good. Although we were so different in character, we had become attached to one another. The daily challenges and combined experiences had forged us into a close-knit unit. Without much communication, we had known exactly what we expected from each other.

And we had crossed thousands of miles of darkest Africa together.

At the moment of separation, Robert seemed overcome by nostalgia. "I wish we could continue this trip forever, Dutchy," he said. "Why do good things always have to end? But just the same, good luck, old boy."

Bill and Frank said their goodbyes together. Shaking hands, Bill had difficulty finding the right words, so the ever-optimistic Frank took charge. He seemed more serious than I had known him throughout the trip. Making it short, he said, "Dutchy, keep fighting. You'll make it. Thanks for being a real mate."

Then all three were gone and once again I was left to my own devices.

Not being British, I couldn't stay for long in this East African colony. Besides, my determination to reach South Africa was stronger than ever.

Obstacles still loomed large. I had no visa for Tanganyika, the next country south; my passport had expired; and I was penniless.

There were only two options: I could travel south by road to Tanganyika, or southeast by rail to Mombasa on the Indian Ocean. The journey by train seemed the most advantageous, for not only could I hop on the train without paying, but there would also be a Dutch consul in Mombasa. He could renew my passport, and in the back of my mind I had visions of ships in the harbor which could surely use a working passenger on the way south.

At the first opportunity, I sneaked on a train. The train was full, so I just stuck my backpack on a rack with the luggage of other passengers.

From there on, my safety would hinge solely on my keeping an eye on the ticket inspector. If I mostly stood in the aisles, it should be easy to stay out of his way.

This plan worked—until I grew careless.

By evening, as the train started its descent toward the Indian Ocean, I proceeded boldly to look for a place to sleep, searching the various coaches for the right spot. Midway in one of the coaches the inspector materialized behind me.

Watching me for a few seconds with keen eyes, he didn't say a word. Somehow I had raised his suspicions. Underestimating the alertness of the British had been my downfall, for about an hour later while I was getting ready for the night in one of the cubicles, he closed in on me like an agent of Scotland Yard.

"Your ticket, young man."

"Sorry, sir," I admitted, hoping honesty might be the best policy, "I haven't got any."

"So I thought," came the dry remark, and with some emphasis, he added, "Better come with me, young man."

There was no escaping on the fast-moving train.

As I followed the inspector sheepishly through the railroad cars, I took in all the details. My mind was instinctively trained to figure a way out of my new dilemma. Showing me into a cubicle where two Marine officers rested on benches, my captor spoke softly but stressed every word, "You stay here, young man, and don't leave this cubicle. Is that clear? I will personally take you to the terminal office in the morning."

With that ominous warning, he went his way, leaving me with my own thoughts.

He had not been rude; apparently, he didn't want to make a scene. Thinking the situation over, I decided not to abandon my original plan of keeping on the rails to Mombasa. It would be easy to slip off the train at one of the smaller railway stations, but then I would probably face more serious difficulties. The inspector would probably inform the police and there would be a search warrant out for me. And with only a few shillings in my pocket, I wouldn't get far.

Taking these realities into consideration, I would be wiser to take a chance that I could evade the inspector at Mombasa. Maybe he would even have some compassion on me and simply forget about a non-paying passenger who was down on his luck.

In the dimly lit cubicle I rested on the floor, covered by my dirty gray blanket. The constant rattling of the steel wheels on the rails was a pleasant melody to me. Listening to the ever-changing sounds, I let my thoughts wander through the African

157

night. Descending from Kenya's highlands, the rail cars curved down in snakelike windings and the wheels of the train squealed and crunched at every bend.

The Marine officers dozed off on either side of me. They also were on the way to Mombasa, where they were to board a freighter. Their snoring was noisy and their breath smelled of liquor, but it didn't bother me. What was important was that I had sleeping room on the hard floor between their benches. But sleep didn't come easily, and I wasn't sure if it was the uncomfortable floor boards or apprehension that kept me awake.

Many people were still asleep when the rosy morning dawned. The landscape had changed. The highlands with their cattle ranges and tea plantations had disappeared. The wide plains where African game still roamed freely had turned into lush hills which looked like the lowlands of the Congo. Among the patches of forest, villages abounded, and coconut palms were everywhere.

Long before the train began to slow, I slipped out of the cubicle and into a vacant toilet a few coaches up from where I was supposed to wait for the inspector. Finally, the train came to a stop. I felt confident when I sneaked out of the odorous toilet and joined the crowd in the passageway.

No sign of the inspector. "He must have more important things to do," I thought, and I was sure he had already forgotten his delinquent passenger.

Colorful Africans, veiled East Indian women, bearded Hindus and Sikhs wearing turbans, and people of European origin milled about. Secure in this multinational crowd, I slowly made for the exit. Although it was only about nine in the morning, the humidity was high and the heat was already bearing down.

Unexpectedly, a few feet from the exit, I came upon the ticket inspector, standing next to two MPs.

"That's him!" the inspector pointed to me.

The nearer MP grabbed me by the arm and demanded, "Documents, please." I showed him my passport, but he was not satisfied.

"You had better come along," he commanded.

I felt the eyes of the thousands of well-behaved citizens of Mombasa staring down the neck of this prisoner of His Majesty.

On a signboard of a one-story building I read the words, "Immigration Office."

"In here," the MP ordered, making me enter the building ahead of him. The wooden structure hadn't seen the services of a maintenance crew in years. The counter exposed numerous splinters where irreverent feet had kicked against the lower panels.

"Someone for you, sir," the MP reported to an officer. "I took him in custody at the railway station. Here's his passport." He saluted stiffly and stepped back into the blazing sun.

The office was staffed by two men. Both wore the white uniform of the tropics. The one in charge was English, the second-in-command was of East Indian descent. The English officer began interrogating me systematically.

"Where are you from?"

"Holland."

"Where are you going?"

"South Africa."

"Can you give me some proof of having booked passage to South Africa?"

"No, I can't. I'm planning to try to work my passage down there," I proposed hopefully.

"In that case, you'll have to leave fifty pounds with me as a guarantee that you will not be a burden to this colony, until you secure your passage."

"I don't have it, sir."

"Then there is no alternative but to ship you off to our local prison," he said stiffly, "until the higher authorities decide what to do with you. No valid passport, no assets, no passage, no valid visa for Kenya! For heaven's sake, young man, why did they ever let you into this colony?"

From the officer's point of view, it was a valid question. How could I possibly explain in a few words the years of suffering—the blood, sweat, and tears I had shed trying to reach South Africa?

159

"Get in that car," he ordered.

"Where are we going?" I asked.

"You'll see when we get there."

I knew these words spelled disaster. My mind reverted to Siegburg. Through the years I had learned not to give in easily.

"Sir, I am a Dutch citizen," I said firmly, "and I demand to see my consul." I had already lost my freedom. What more could be jeopardized by seeing the consul?

Sitting in the officer's small car with my backpack on my knees, I studied the surroundings intently to see if we were approaching anything that resembled a jail. But true to my request, the British official drove up to the Dutch consul's office.

"You go in first and explain your case," he said. "I'll join you later." He stationed himself in front of the door.

The office I entered was small, scantily furnished, and hot. No secretary or typist was in sight, but the Dutch consul himself was. He was about sixty years old with a calm face and quiet manner.

"May I help you?" he asked, looking at me over the rim of his glasses. Though his manner did not betray it, I was sure I made a poor impression. My worn clothes, unshaven face, and shabby backpack could not have generated much respect. But pretending a dignity I did not feel, I asked, "Could you renew my passport, sir?" and placed the little booklet on his desk.

"Of course, I can," he replied pleasantly. Turning to the right page, he started filling out the required lines.

"On what ship are you traveling, Mr. Vandenberg?"

"So far I've come overland, sir," I said. "I am on my way to South Africa and have used every available means of transportation to get this far—my feet, trucks, dugout canoes, and trains."

"You don't mean it!" he exclaimed, looking incredulous.

"I certainly do!" I said. "Take a look at my passport; it will give you the true picture."

"Is that immigration officer waiting outside for you?"

"That's correct, sir." In a few short sentences, I tried to bring the Dutch consul up to date on my unpleasant circum-

160

stances. I did not get a chance to finish my explanations, for the impatient immigration officer knocked hard on the door and then walked into the office. Pointing to me, he addressed the consul, saying, "Have you already decided what to do with this individual?"

"What do you mean, what am I going to do with him?" the consul replied calmly. "This man has a valid passport and a valid transit visa for Kenya."

"Valid! Valid!" the Briton shouted. "Who decides what is valid around here? I do! This man doesn't have a penny. People like that don't belong in this colony; they ought to be locked up."

By now the British official sounded irrational.

Fortunately, the Dutch consul took the initiative. Speaking to me, he said, "Mr. Vandenberg, please wait outside for a moment. I want to have a private word with this officer. Just leave your passport on my desk, for safety's sake."

Standing with my ear to the door, I listened carefully to the conversation. My fate was going to be decided by these two officials and I wanted to be in on it.

After a few nonessentials, both parties came to the point. I overheard the Dutch consul ask, "How much do you want to keep him out of jail? Give me a figure."

"Fifty pounds sterling, no less," the British immigration officer replied, "and that only on the condition that you will keep his passport until he is out of the country."

"That's fine. Leave the rest to me."

The conference lasted another ten minutes. Then the door opened and the representative of the British crown walked by, contentedly folding a check and putting it in his pocket. Passing in front of me, he looked straight ahead as if I were not even there.

It was my turn again to face the Dutch consul. Looking at me with a smile, he said, "That little agreement cost me fifty pounds, just to keep you out of jail. In accordance with international law, that sum will be reimbursed to me as soon as you have left the country. In the meantime, I must hold on to your passport, Mr. Vandenberg. I owe that to myself. As far as your traveling is concerned, the only way you can get out of Kenya will be by ship. The immigration people would never allow you to continue overland. But leave it to me; I might get you on board a freighter going south."

It was difficult to find the proper words to express my gratitude. "Thank you so much for bailing me out, sir," I said. "If you had not intervened, I would now be a prisoner in some British fortress. At least this way, I'm out of the frying pan."

"But not yet in the fire!" the sympathetic consul said.

Chapter Ten

THE GRAND FINALE

At five in the morning, aboard the coaster *Sandman* on the Indian Ocean, I stood on deck and thrilled in my heart as thousands of tiny lights rose on the horizon. There was no moon, which made the lights even brighter and more inviting.

I had left Europe nearly two years ago, and finally, stretched in front of me, lay the embodiment of my dreams: South Africa, the goal I had pursued day after day. Those twinkling lights on the horizon were the lights of Durban.

I wanted to shout, "I made it! I made it!" but restrained myself. Yet a sensation of victory, a feeling of absolute happiness surged through me. Many times I had longed for this moment, and often while in some hopeless situation, I had doubted that I would ever live to see it.

Some whose paths I had crossed on the vast African continent had labeled me a lunatic. No money, no transportation, no valid papers. It was impossible! "He's crazy! Out of his mind!"

Perhaps. But freedom burns more deeply in the heart of the man from whom freedom has been taken.

Leaning on the ship's rail, my eyes remained glued to that strip of inviting land which was South Africa.

The ship docked in early morning, and as soon as the gangplank was lowered, an immigration official came aboard. The *Sandman* was primarily a freighter, and besides myself she carried only three other European immigrants. In a businesslike manner, the passports and visas of the three other immigrants were checked and okayed. They could make themselves a new home.

With a lightness in my heart and a smile on my lips, I proudly handed the officer my passport. The indifferent look on his face did not change as he flipped through the pages.

"I *cannot* grant you permission to enter the Union of South Africa," he said. "First, we were not forewarned of your arrival. Secondly, you have a visa in your passport which means absolutely nothing to me."

I could not believe my ears. My joy turned instantly to dismay and I felt myself getting red hot and then ice cold. I could not utter a word. I wanted to say something, but nothing came from my lips.

The immigration officer turned to the captain of the *Sandman*, who had been a silent witness, and said coldly, "Obviously, I do not have to tell you, captain, to keep an eye on this man. Under the circumstances, we cannot give him a landing permit, so you will have to take him back to Holland."

At that, I found my voice. "B-b-but, sir, l-l-listen just a moment. Just a few minutes," I stammered, "that's all I need to explain everything to you."

I was more desperate than I had ever been.

"I am sorry," the officer said. "I have no time. I have important business to attend to." His words struck me a devastating blow. He picked up his attache case, strode across the ship's deck, and disappeared down the gangplank.

I felt as if my feet were nailed to the deck. This couldn't be true. This could not be my reward for trying so hard. I *must* be dreaming. This could only be a nightmare. But when I turned in despair to the captain and looked into his face, I knew I wasn't dreaming.

He looked at me with the eyes of a man who had been double-crossed. His face was clear enough for me to read his mind—and he was thinking, "You louse! You just had to pull this trick on my ship, didn't you?"

He motioned to the boatswain: "Bos'n, don't let this guy out of your sight. He is not allowed to leave the ship and we must take him back to Holland."

For emphasis he added, "Remember, I'm holding you responsible. Is that understood?"

He spoke not a word to me. He simply gave me a penetrating look, then walked away, shrugging his shoulders.

Inside, I was empty, as if life itself had betrayed me.

The boatswain trailed me like a faithful dog, but we hardly exchanged a word.

Within minutes word spread around the *Sandman* and every sailor talked about the "illegal" immigrant. I acted as if I didn't notice how the boatswain kidded with the other sailors who passed by. I continued to look at the promised land, though I shouldn't have thought of it as "promised" anymore. Not for me. I was only supposed to look at it.

That day was the longest I had ever lived. I went to bed feeling sheer, uncontrollable resentment. During the night, though, my anger subsided and I awakened alert and thinking. I had thwarted difficulty before; why not again? New plans began to take shape.

The boatswain occupied the berth opposite me. He smoked one cigarette after the other, and between clouds of blue-gray smoke, he squinted in my direction.

Reviewing my life from my horizontal position, it seemed I had been desperately trying to defuse bombs wherever I went for the last seven years. With closed eyes, I could see some of my prisoner friends who had tried to escape from Siegburg. Those who were recaptured had to spend at least fourteen days in solitary confinement. As further punishment, they were forced into what some SS guards sarcastically called *Himmelfahrts Kommando* (Ascension Commando). Those prisoners had the "honor" of defusing Allied bombs which failed to explode on impact. Their guards stood at a safe distance, and if the prisoners succeeded in dismantling the bomb, everyone was happy. But when the bomb exploded, only the guards were happy; the prisoners were blown to smithereens.

How I could identify with those men! Wasn't that what I had been doing for years? Defusing bombs? Dismantling one dangerous situation after another? Castor had been a dangerous bomb, but thank God he was successfully defused. So was the SS guard in Siegburg who got me on the list to "extermination somewhere else." The Sahara was a huge bomb, but thank goodness, it was dismantled and was now a thing of the past. The immigration officer in Mombasa, the various diseases, the police, the Congo—all passed in review. Offhand, I could think of at least three dozen persons, places, or situations which had been like threatening bombs. They had caused havoc and anxiety at the time, but most had failed to explode on impact. So far, all had been successfully defused.

Now I faced one last bomb. Was this the one that would blow *me* to smithereens? I would have to tackle this one head-on. I would have to look death squarely in the face—for deportation would mean death to my dream.

When the faint, rosy glow of dawn finally announced the new day, I heard quiet snoring from the other berth. The boatswain's need for sleep was more powerful than his responsibility to watch me.

I waited, extremely alert. His snoring became louder and more regular.

Carefully, I got up. The boatswain continued to sleep. In only my socks, I sneaked to the door. It seemed to take an eternity before I was able to open the heavy door without any noise.

The deck of the vessel was deserted. No, not altogether! Close to the gangplank stood a South African black in uniform. He was probably placed there to keep an eye out for thieves. Or could he have been there for other reasons? I had to take a chance.

Nonchalantly, I walked toward the gangway, greeted the guard with a friendly, "Hello," and walked down to the quay. The hard pavement felt like velvet under my feet, but I didn't dare run yet, for I was still in sight of the man in uniform.

The day had just begun and the streets of Durban were still deserted. I walked for quite a while without having a special goal, happy to put a considerable distance between the *Sandman* and me. All the time my brain was a hub of activity. What could I do? Where should I go from here?

Every idea that occurred to me, I had to reject. I had arrived in the country of my dreams. I had realized my goal after tremendous setbacks and almost insurmountable problems, but I was forced to walk the pavement as an undesirable immigrant, a penniless prospect for the South African police files. Just the same, I longed to stay in this country. I had fought too long and too hard to get here.

When these facts were clear, a bright thought surfaced: Why not go to the local immigration office and ask for an interview with the highest official in town? What did I have to lose? All I needed was an understanding soul who had time to listen to me. After all, the British Consul in Algeria had given me an entry permit for this country, even though the officials here might not recognize its validity.

In the course of the morning—a little nervous but with my mind made up—I entered the immigration office. As luck would have it, the first man I encountered was the officer who had refused my entry the previous day.

"Of all the nerve!" he exploded. "You! Here! What are you trying to prove?" His steel blue eyes shot fire. "Didn't I give explicit orders that under no circumstances you should disembark?"

Hurriedly, I tried to explain. "It's like this, sir," I said. "In your eyes, I may be an illegal immigrant, but believe me, I have struggled for years to get to this country. Now I am asking you the right to explain my plight to the highest authority in this office and let him decide what to do with me."

Somehow my words penetrated. At least the officer listened.

"Well, if you have made up your mind that you want to face the music," he said in a surly tone, "the consequences are yours."

Visibly impressed with his own importance, he grabbed my arm and took me to the second floor. He opened a door and I looked over his shoulder into a large office. Five men worked behind desks. They wore the same uniform as the officer, who now pushed me deeper into the lion's den.

"Here's the man I spoke to you about yesterday," he addressed one of the officers who had more gold on his sleeves than the others.

167

The officer in charge looked up. He had an austere but sympathetic expression. His hair was slightly gray at the temples.

"Let's see what kind of a case this is," he said to the officer who brought me in. Looking right through me, he said, "As I understand it, you do not possess a valid visa to land here. Why don't you?"

"Sir, will you allow me about a quarter of an hour to explain my case and to defend myself?" I asked. "It is impossible to do this in a couple of seconds."

"Go ahead," he said. "Speak up."

As I spoke, my nerves became less tense. "Sir, I was only twenty-two years old when I made up my mind to emigrate to South Africa two years ago. I started without money, or visas, or anything at all that would make it easy for me to get here, but I did have my own two feet. I didn't have any illusions, either. From my eighteenth year, I was kept four years in prisons and concentration camps. The reason was that I had tried to reach England during the war to join the Dutch Free Forces. Only with a certain amount of hope in my heart did I begin this trip to South Africa."

As I described my adventures of the last two years, one by one the other four officers stopped their work and joined the officer in charge to listen to the tales of this strange Dutchman.

It had been nearly an hour since I began my story, and I sensed that I was winning ground. With increased enthusiasm, I pleaded my case.

"Gentlemen, you have just heard about some of the rough passages of my life. Right now, I am twenty-four years old, and so far I have never yet led a normal life. Only the hope of reaching this country kept me going. During the last seven years, I have been kicked around and beaten up; typhoid, malaria, and sunstroke have ravaged my body; I have been tracked and chased like a wild beast. The atrocities of the Nazi war camps still haunt me. The French jailed me in Algeria. The Foreign Legion kept me in its claws. The British had me arrested in Kenya. Not any of you probably know what devastating effects the things I have just mentioned can have on a human being, but in spite of everything, I have remained convinced all these years that some day I would be allowed the right to live in a country of my own choice.

"I have fought to get here with the most bitter determination I could muster," I concluded, "and thanks to God alone, I have persisted. I have persisted to the very end—until I got here. It is now up to you either to throw me out, or to give me a chance to live here in the land I have dreamed of for so long."

The office was as quiet as the dead of night. The men in uniform looked at one another without saying a word. Then the officer with the graying hair got up, held out his hand toward me and said, not without emotion, "Mr. Vandenberg, welcome to your new Fatherland!"

The other officers nodded in approval.

A hard, rumbling echo thundered through my body and soul.

Welcome to your new Fatherland! Welcome! Welcome!

Chapter Eleven

A NEW BEGINNING

After a few years of trying my hand at various jobs, I joined the Trans African Safari Company as a guide. My responsibility was to take the rich and adventurous on tours of the African continent, wherever they wanted to go. In this manner, in a comfort I had never known on the road, I saw the remainder of Africa's magnificence.

How marvelous and exhilarating life had become. Time has a perfect way of healing old wounds. However deep the physical and psychological damage of the war years and my time in transit had been, my many months of roaming Africa as a guide had obliterated all ill feelings. I was able to remember the pleasant moments of those days and eradicate the evil memories.

My sister emigrated from Holland to South Africa and made her home in Johannesburg where my headquarters were. At my sister's home, I met one of her friends, a dark-haired, lovely woman named Connie. We began to date, and soon I realized she was the girl with whom I wanted to spend the rest of my life. I asked her to marry me and was overjoyed when she accepted my proposal.

I was thirty years old and ready to settle down. I quit my job as a safari guide and took work as a commercial artist in Johannesburg.

God blessed our union with four wonderful children: Ingrid, Yvonne, and André, who shared our adventures the rest of the time we stayed in Africa, and later in America, a fourth child came to us—Marianne.

Soon after Connie and I were married, I managed to close an open chapter of my life. Going to my car one day after work in Johannesburg, I found a note behind one of the windshield wipers:

> Saw you coming out of your car this morning, Dutchy. If you would like to, call me at this number.
>
> —Dolly of the *Desert Rat*

What can she be up to? I wondered. Maybe I can find out what happened to Castor.

The only member of the *Desert Rat* I had met since our Sahara days was Dan. On one of my safaris to Kenya, I had found my faithful friend settled in an uninteresting job in Nairobi. For some unknown reason, the fire seemed to have gone out of him. There was no spark in our meeting, and it was apparent that the years of separation had eroded our closeness.

It would be interesting to find out how the rest of the original party had fared. A few days later, Connie and I met Dolly at her apartment. To my amazement, Ann, Dolly's mother, was also there.

"And Castor," I asked, "whatever happened to him?"

Dolly reported that Castor had ditched James after the Sahara crossing, and to crown his evil-doing, had put her in a house of prostitution in Lagos, Nigeria. He needed money badly, and vice offered the easiest way to make a fast buck. Fortunately, her predicament did not last long, for a young Englishman heard of Dolly's plight and came to her rescue.

"*He* got me out," Dolly said with enthusiasm, "and would you believe I fell in love with him and he with me? His name is Rick and he is now my husband."

Dolly and Rick had settled in Nigeria. But Castor wanted to push on to South Africa. He forced Ann to go with him, and both finally arrived by ship in Cape Town.

Once in South Africa, Castor soon grew tired of Ann and discarded her like a dirty rag. She had served his purposes.

Poor Ann, I thought. Even for her who had supplied most of the money for the trans-Africa trip, the outcome had been one of great disappointment.

"What is your latest information on Castor?" I asked.

"Rick and I only came to this country recently," Dolly said. "We took my mother to live with us. The last we heard about my stepfather was that some time ago he was severely beaten by a group of Basutu men. How he fared after that, we do not know. We don't even know if he lived or died of the beating."

I never heard of Castor again.

As our family increased, we moved to Salisbury, Rhodesia (now Zimbabwe) and I started a business in wall and floor tiling.

I felt as if I had completed my most strenuous physical journey, but now I faced an even more important one: my spiritual journey.

My interest in spiritual things was at a low ebb. Not that I doubted the existence of an eternal God. How could I? I could so clearly call to memory those days I lay on the concrete floor in Siegburg, my body wasted, all hope and memory gone, unaware of my whereabouts or even of my own name. I had looked eternity in the face, and after crying out to God, had been saved from death.

In retrospect, I could see God's invisible hand upon me through all those years on the African trails. And now, married to a wonderful woman, the years had turned to physical sweetness.

Yet what had I done about the promise I made to God in the depths of my despair? My vow had been genuine—but I had done nothing to fulfill it.

I had noticed my moral standards slipping these last few years. I cursed like a sailor and could work up a temper at the slightest provocation. As drinking and smoking were not then recognized as vices, not even by many churches, I felt free to indulge in these habits wholeheartedly. It was obvious to me that a decadence had set in, but I didn't know how to stop it. Periodically I would quit smoking my normal sixty to ninety cigarettes a day, but I always fell back into the practice.

I felt contaminated spiritually but didn't recognize the source. My mind was corrupt, but the agent which polluted it was invisible.

Early in our marriage, we had decided to bring up our children the "right" way. In our book that meant we must take them to church every Sunday. The church we chose was orthodox and prided itself on correct doctrine. It preached the laws of God, but love was often absent.

I presumed that the pew warmers I saw in church came out of habit. Or did these people really know God? Were they perhaps tuned in on a higher frequency than I was?

A year after we started going to church, I was asked to be a deacon. That elevated me one step over the churchgoers. But as an unfit, spiritually blind deacon, I was not capable of helping anyone. In my heart there remained an emptiness that a higher position in the church could not fill. A gnawing uncertainty ate at my soul and the inner conflicts raged on. Though I didn't realize it, the Holy Spirit of God was preparing ground.

One Sunday evening, my wife stayed home to look after our children and I went to church alone. After the service, the pastor asked the deacons to stay and pray. The only difficulty was that I *could not pray*. Here I was, a respected deacon in the church, and I could not utter aloud a simple prayer. Something was seriously wrong. I went outside and stepped into the car, very conscious of a heavy weight in my heart. I had a deep need that I didn't know how to deal with. I bowed my head and just sat. I knew God existed, but how could He be pleased with a life like mine?

After fourteen years of freedom, I was less prepared to meet God than when I was a body of skin-covered bones.

What freedom!

As our pastor had recited the laws of God that morning— "You shall not serve other Gods; you shall not steal; you shall not lie; you shall not commit adultery; you shall not jealously desire the property of others"—I sadly concluded that I had violated every one of them. Now, I started to pray and kept praying from the depths of my heart.

"God, forgive me," I prayed. "Jesus, forgive all my wrong living, all my failures." I didn't know what else to say, but I meant business. "God, forgive me. Jesus, forgive me my sins. Jesus, forgive me!"

Instantly, I experienced something very strange. I felt as if I was standing under a shower, dirty and covered with grime, and the shower was doing a thorough job of cleansing me.

Then a wonderful joy gripped my soul and a heavenly peace settled over me.

I couldn't grasp what was happening, and tried to shrug it off. Jesus was indeed answering my prayer, taking away my sins and guilt! Why had no one ever told me this was possible? Why hadn't anyone ever shared with me that I could be forgiven and *know* it? No one had ever explained to me that repentance was the prerequisite of a cleaned-up life. Never had I read about a real conversion, except in the pages of the New Testament.

Arriving home, I couldn't explain to my wife what had taken place. But I knew that the God who had answered my prayer in a German death camp had also answered my prayer in Rhodesia and had performed a miracle in my soul.

About this time, we were told in church that an evangelist from the United States would be visiting us in Rhodesia. The meetings were to be held in a big tent on the outskirts of town. I didn't know what an evangelist was supposed to do. Even the name of the evangelist, Billy Graham, didn't mean much to most of us.

In a week of preaching in the large tent, Mr. Graham gave us the crystal-clear facts of how Jesus Christ had dealt with the real problem in the world. Whether or not we wanted to recognize it, disobedience to God—or sin—had pervaded all people. Sin had wrecked and defiled my life and the lives of everyone around me.

Not only did Mr. Graham show us the cause of human wretchedness, he also showed us the cure. Perfect and complete healing was to be found in Jesus Christ. He just quoted Jesus, who had plainly said, "I am the way and the truth and the life. No one comes to the Father except through me" (John 14:6). I knew of many people trying out different ways, but God had only made one way available: Jesus!

Mr. Graham made sure that we all realized *what* Jesus came to do in this sick world when he stressed Jesus' own statement in Luke 19:10: "For the Son of Man came to seek and to save what was lost."

How about all that evil, the many soiled lives, the mountains of sin that we were all guilty of? Billy Graham again went to the Bible for God's answer and read from Isaiah 1:18: "'Come now, let us reason together,' says the Lord. 'Though your sins are like scarlet, they shall be as white as snow; though they are red as crimson, they shall be like wool.'"

Of course I had heard or read these statements before, but apparently they had made no impact on me. Now, I could fully identify. I had been a faker, like many others. Someone who had an imaginary religion, without realizing it.

The same God who had saved the husk of my body in a wartime prison camp had now saved my soul, the real me.

The night Billy Graham preached, my wife and I surrendered our lives to Jesus Christ. We had no idea what would be in store for us. That was of no importance right then. The glorious truth was that God through Jesus had forgiven us and had given us a new start, a new beginning with Him.

We had been given a new beginning that would eventually lead to an eternal fatherland.

EPILOGUE

Neither André nor Connie Vandenberg knew that the other had gone forward to answer Billy Graham's call that evening. André was a counselor and was sitting in a different place than Connie. Both of them, however, have never wavered from the commitment they made that night.

But the winds of change were sweeping over the great African continent André had come to love. He sensed that the self-rule movement would bring difficult times in the coming years. There would be more distrust, more hatred, and increased bloodshed among the races.

André and Connie would like to have stayed, but what kind of future could they expect for their children?

So in 1961, a year after the Graham crusade, André brought his family to the United States. He was thirty-seven years old.

Through a light haze the famous Statue of Liberty came into view on that cold April morning. Almost everyone on deck felt a great exhilaration. Many of the passengers were refugees for whom the thrill of arriving in the land of the free brought great happiness.

As the ship docked, the Vandenberg family looked up with awe at the skyscrapers of New York. The jungles of Africa had appeared much more inviting to André than this one.

As the Vandenbergs passed through immigration, an officer glanced at the three children, then looked at André with approval and said, "Coming to the States was the best thing you could have done for your children."

At that point, André was not so sure.

As they walked through Manhattan, the Vandenbergs felt dwarfed by the superstructures of concrete and steel. A quick look around convinced them that these surroundings were not going to be theirs. André felt that the hustle and bustle of man and machine would drive a nature-lover like him to an early grave.

The next day André purchased an old station wagon, loaded up the family and their belongings, and headed for California. Settling for a while in San Diego, the Vandenbergs began attending a Dutch Reformed Church. They soon discovered that the church did not satisfy their needs. André was hungry to get more of the Lord, and to have the power of the Spirit in his life.

"When he was in the concentration camp," said his youngest daughter, Marianne, "he promised to serve the Lord, but when he got out he didn't know how to go about it. He wanted to do it, but it was like he was so ignorant about how."

André moved his family to Santa Barbara and took employment as superintendent of buildings and grounds at Westmont College. A friend talked the Vandenbergs into attending Calvary Baptist Church, and André heard a lot there that he had never heard about the Bible. That's when he really began to grow in the Lord. He also began to fulfill his promise to God: He began to preach in rescue missions and jails. He ministered individually to the students and many in the college came to know the Lord through André.

The years were good to the Vandenbergs. The children grew and the family prospered. André had a good job, and soon the family bought its own home.

But there were great changes on the horizon. A Dutch friend named Hank van Galen and André had developed an idea for agricultural self-help programs in underdeveloped nations. Van Galen felt that while they helped people in those countries develop their agriculture, they would have an open ear for the gospel of Jesus Christ. They called this outreach "Twofold Harvest."

Hank telephoned André one day from his headquarters in North Carolina: "Would you like to come over and help us?"

Both André and Connie had good jobs. All of their children were in school, and the family was happily settled. If they agreed to join Twofold Harvest, they had no idea where in the world they would end up. There appeared to be more obstacles than the change seemed to justify, and André wavered.

Hundreds of thoughts ran pell-mell through his head. The material and spiritual poverty in the world was colossal and out of proportion. Most people in the United States lived in luxury compared to those in developing nations. And what great spiritual opportunity there was in the United States! Everyone could turn on the radio or television and hear the claims of Jesus Christ. Few of those in developing nations could do so. Most people in the United States could get an education or a job, while the availability of those things in developing countries was inadequate.

Other reasons made André hesitate. He was fifty-one years old. His family had deep roots in the community in which they lived. But then, he reasoned, if God wanted him to serve in another country, who was he to refuse?

The Vandenbergs prayed about the offer and decided to tell Hank van Galen that they would join him within a few months. Uncertainty plagued André from time to time. Was he doing the right thing—uprooting his family; giving up the security of home and job? Did God indeed want him to go at his age and work for Twofold Harvest?

Or was it perhaps his own will and personal desire? Did he have an unconscious, ulterior motive?

Since he was not sure of the answers to these questions, he prayed. How could he possibly know God's direction in this move that not only would alter the course of his own life but touch the lives of his children as well?

It was often André's experience that, when he was alone with God, the answers to his questions had come. This time, he knew God would not fail him. With deep concern over whether he was taking the right step, he prayed on his knees one night, pleading with God to honor someone else with the job.

"Lord," he prayed, "You know that my knowledge is so limited. There are so many other people who have a better education. I'm sure many others in this world are better suited for this job. So many know more than I do, Lord. Please send one who has more qualifications than I have."

As André prayed, he saw in his mind the scene where our Savior was about to feed the five thousand. A large crowd was gathered. Then very unexpectedly a voice came to André, distinctly asking, "Do you think the boy who gave the five loaves and two fishes was the only one who had food with him?"

It was a question André had never before considered, and it made him examine Jesus' miracle from a different angle.

He reviewed the story he knew so well. Out of all those people present at the feeding of the five thousand, would there have been only one young boy smart enough to bring food along? How about all the men and women? Surely there were others who had packed a lunch that day.

After thinking the matter through, André answered, "Lord, I think there must have been others who had some provisions they could have shared, but it seemed that the boy was the only one who was willing to give all he had."

Then the Lord impressed upon André's heart: "I want you to be like that boy. It was because that boy was willing to give all he had that my name was glorified and others were helped."

André was astounded. He heard the voice no more, and the picture faded away. Still in communion with the Lord, he came to realize that it didn't really matter if others knew more than he did; nor whether others were younger than he; nor whether they could give more than he could give. It didn't matter if some had an educational degree and he didn't. All of this was not of the least importance to the Lord. The Lord was looking for someone like the boy, who was willing to give his all.

The uncertainty was gone. André had received his marching orders. He knew that God would take care of the future.

The Vandenbergs settled in the mountains of North Carolina, outside Asheville. André's yearning to help others help themselves, and to help them find the Lord, became increasingly stronger.

On visits to Holland, André had been saddened by the religious formalism that had taken over his homeland. It hurt him to see that same evolution taking place in the United States, where people enjoyed God's great bounty more than in any other land. He was frustrated to see people who had been inundated with the Gospel become so cold and distant to the reality of Jesus Christ. He began to search for places where people were truly hungry for the gospel.

This led André to seven years of work among the *campesinos* of Honduras. On the shores of Lake Yojoa, André and Hank van Galen implemented a Twofold Harvest program through which they helped families build decent housing, organized and built a school, and began agricultural programs designed to improve irrigation. Also at this time, André preached in a small village nearby, and by the grace of God started a church.

Twofold Harvest was tremendously rewarding for André as long as he could work directly with the people. As the people of Lake Yojoa became self-sufficient André moved on to a Twofold Harvest outreach in Haiti.

In both Honduras and Haiti, Connie worked side by side with André, and often they wondered, particularly after a dark day, whether they were doing enough—sometimes whether they were doing any good at all. "Are we getting through to these people?" they asked themselves; and they could not truly answer the question.

One day in Honduras, an old woman came to the door of the Vandenberg home and said, "We missed you so much before you came here." What finer confirmation of their work could they have found!

André found his greatest sense of the fulfillment of God's plan in his life during his second stint in Honduras, the one that ended with his death.

This venture was sponsored and financed by the Vandenbergs' home church, the Naples Baptist Church of Naples, North Carolina. In March of 1987, André took Connie and five others from the Naples Church to Honduras to help build Sunday school rooms for a church. That trip sparked a tremendous urge in André to go back to Honduras, and over the next few months all those who made the trip felt that the Lord wanted them to begin a ministry there.

They went back to Honduras to look over two potential sites for a mission. They checked out the availability and cost of land, what churches were already in existence, and what specific needs the people had. A Dutch woman who lived in the village of Lagas offered to sell her house and nursery to the church, and the Naples church determined that this was God's will and provision for them.

André and Connie went to Honduras in May of 1988 and established themselves in Lagas. They moved into the Dutch woman's house and started a village church there, meeting in their home until they could build a church building. The church decided to keep the nursery business operational, so that a few families at least would have work there. The business prospered and André was happy with that. He put all the profits back into the nursery, putting more local people to work. He felt that this not only helped the local economy but also helped men be better fathers, providing for their families.

André had no problem with the language; he was a linguist. He already spoke half a dozen languages fluently, and a dozen others well enough to get by. He had learned to speak Creole in Haiti.

Lagas was about three hours from the coast, in a mountainous region north of Tegucigalpa. The mountains reached upward to 18,000 feet. The village lay at a lower elevation, in a tropical area.

There were several other villages nearby, and André visited all of them. He spent much time walking around, sharing the Gospel. Hardly anybody passed who didn't receive a tract and a good word. Many were illiterate people with whom André took the time to work through the tract.

His favorite tract was entitled, "How To Get Rich."

He would meet someone on the trail and start up a conversation.

"Do you read?" André would ask.

"Yes! I read."

"Well, I've got something here—'How To Get Rich.'"

That got their attention.

"Oh, but it's not the money richness I'm talking about," André would say. "It is something far better than that."

He led many people to believe in Jesus Christ as Lord and Savior.

André was at his best when he could share one on one, but he also founded churches in three nearby villages.

"There were tons of children in those places," Connie said, "children who desperately needed the Gospel. The growth of the churches and of the mission there has been astounding. Such a need! People are so hungry for the Word. There were places where people had never heard a clear presentation of the Gospel. That's what overwhelmed us. People would walk an hour and a half over those steep mountains to get to the services."

André used every opportunity to minister. He had a Bible study each morning at 6:30 with the workers in the nursery. Many of those laborers came to know the Lord and are now church leaders.

One of the workers was Pepe, a Roman Catholic. Pepe listened to the Bible study each morning, and one morning he challenged André on a point. "Yes," he said, "that's what your Bible says."

The next time André went to town, he bought a Catholic Bible and took it with him the next day to the Bible study.

"Now, Pepe," he said, "today we are going to teach out of *your* Bible."

He showed the group that the message of salvation is the same in the Catholic as in the Protestant Bible. Pepe and his whole family came to know the Lord, and all are faithful in the church today.

"In worldly things," said Ingrid, "my father was a poor man, but he got his enjoyment out of the very simple things in life— and from his work for the Lord."

One of his grandchildren said, "When I think of 'Opa,' I think of him reading his Bible." André never watched television; he spent his idle time reading the Word.

"My earliest memories of him," said Marianne, "are of him sitting on the couch reading his Bible. He had a favorite seat on the couch."

André had a natural affinity with the people among whom he ministered. Times were hard and life was tough in the mountains of Honduras, but André Vandenberg was accustomed to such things. He had survived for four years in the Nazi concentration camp. He had survived the long journey from Holland to South Africa. He was a tough man.

In May of 1989, after a year in Honduras, André came home to North Carolina. He had been having hard pains in his chest, but a thorough check by physicians showed no cause for alarm.

He had lost twenty pounds, however, and that concerned his family.

Marianne hugged him one day and said, "Now, Dad, you're going to have to slow down."

"Yes, yes," he answered, "but there is so much to do, and so little time."

André Vandenberg returned once more to Honduras, where so much work awaited him.

On the day of his death, he led the four men from Kansas to the foot of the mountain leading up to the village they sought.

He looked up the mountain.

"One more mountain," he said, and as he had done so many times before, he put his left foot in front of his right and began to climb it.

Bob Terrell